My Story—Jonathan B Taylor

My Story:

Strewn Along the Highway

By

Jonathan B. Taylor

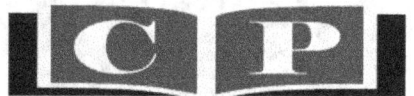

Cadmus Publishing

CadmusPublishing.com

My Story—Jonathan B Taylor

MY STORY: STREWN ALONG THE HIGHWAY

Manufactured in the United States of America. Copyright 2025 by Jonathan B. Taylor   All rights reserved. No part of this book may be reproduced in any form, audio, digital, or in print, except excerpts by reviewers, without written permission from the copyright holder or Cadmus Publishing LLC.

DISCLAIMER:
   The thoughts, opinions, and expressions herein are those of the author and do not reflect those of Cadmus Publishing LLC. Any similarities to actual events or people are purely coincidental. Names and distinguishing characteristics may have been changed to preserve the identities of any individuals. Published by Cadmus Publishing LLC. P. O. Box 8664. Haledon, NJ 07538

Web: Cadmuspublishing.com
Business email: admin@cadmuspublishing.com
ISBN# 978-1-63751-335-4

   Book Catalog Info Categories:
   Autobiography

Cadmus Publishing
CadmusPublishing.com

My Story—Jonathan B Taylor

My Story

While some may wind their way carelessly through comfortable, easy lives, others will work our way through more treacherous trails and where one soul may soften, another will grow strong. Cast into an arena to be pitted against ruthless, unfeeling foes, I've found myself tested to the limits of what the human spirit may endure but, regardless of whether one is here to learn a lesson or for final exams, we all have a story to tell and this one is mine. I'm actually telling just a small fragment of the story but sometimes the smallest fragments can have the greatest impact and provide the most revealing pieces to a puzzle.

My story is unusual, which can raise walls of doubt in people's minds, surrounding it in speculation. Within those walls, the story's confusing subject matter creates a twisted labyrinth through, which some may find the tale hard to follow. These things have made it difficult to translate my story into words and even more difficult to relate through an abstraction but I think that those who follow it to the end will ultimately find it interesting when they've emerged on the other side.

For some there will be no doubt or speculation. Their familiarity with the backdrop of this story will allow the pieces to fall easily into

My Story—Jonathan B Taylor

place. They are the viewers and players who have watched it all unravel before their eyes. Maintaining a harsh silence and feigning a clumsy ignorance have made them crucial accessories to the crime. By pulling on the puppet strings like playful children, these thoughtless collaborators fell to their knees and kissed the feet of a man they have never met or seen, becoming his dutiful servants and fiendish accomplices, oblivious to the sticky strings that pulled on their own heads and hands.

My story is titled 'Strewn along the Highway' and I hope that whoever reads this, whether they're familiar with the back story or hearing it all for the first time, will pause for a moment and listen to what I have to say. If you do venture down this rabbit hole, the trip requires an open mind so anyone who is packing tunnel vision should probably check it at the door or else they'll never make it past the first paragraph.

For those who make the journey and follow the spiral to the end, I am grateful for your time and effort. This is a story that needs to be told and if reaching its conclusion leaves you hanging with questions and conjecture, then I will do my best to provide the answers and explanations that you seek by having a dialogue about my story with whoever is interested in exploring it further.

My Story—Jonathan B Taylor

The following is an affidavit. It is a written statement of facts pertaining to a particular sequence of events, which provides a narrative with a disjointed and sporadic tale. This is an account of my experience with suppressed memories that I found myself reliving in 1989, when the lost images gained buoyancy and appeared at the surface of my consciousness. As the misplaced scenes from my past flashed on the screen, a story began to unfold, uncovering the answer to a mystery, which I have never revealed until now.

My Story—Jonathan B Taylor

Foreword:

The emergence of resurfaced memories first began for me in the early spring of 1989 when I suddenly recalled an encounter that I had with an individual named Paul Pothier, Jr. who I met while attending a party in the town of Fairhaven, MA. During that encounter, Paul told me that he was the 15-year-old son of Mary Beth Vickers who was a friend and former co-worker of mine that I had worked with at a printed circuit board manufacturing company called E.P.E.C. Inc. in the New Bedford Industrial Park. He also told me that he hadn't spoken to his mother in years and asked me to relay the message that he wanted to see her.

For reasons that were unclear to me at the time, I had no memory of meeting Paul in the days that immediately followed the encounter and it wasn't until several days later that I started to recall fragments of our conversation, beginning with the message for his mother. As the memory of our meeting slowly resurfaced, I went to see Mary Beth to relay Paul's message. I then went in search of Paul to let him know that I had spoken to his mother and that she wanted to see him too. It was during this time that I began to recall additional details of my conversation with Paul from that night, which had previously eluded me. I saw flashes of him telling me that we were brothers and

My Story—Jonathan B Taylor

that Mary Beth was my mother too. He then said that I had been hypnotized as a child in order to conceal this information from me.

Unfortunately, I was unable to reconnect with Paul but I did speak to Mary Beth again and asked her about Paul's astonishing statements. When I asked her if she was in fact my mother, she responded by saying that it wasn't her place to tell me and I needed to talk to my parents because they were the only ones who had the right to tell me that information. The next time I spoke with Mary Beth, she told me she had talked to her son Paul and that he told her he was never at any party, which I knew wasn't true because I had already confirmed Paul's presence at the party with others who were there. She then accused me of making the whole thing up and said that she wanted nothing more to do with me. At first, I was taken aback by her sudden change in demeanor but as more memories made their way to the surface, an explanation for her odd behavior slowly came into view.

Over the next few months, Paul's initial revelation kicked off a tsunami of resurfaced memories that overwhelmed me with a fresh new batch of vivid images each day. Amid the steady stream of recovered recollections were some key encounters with certain individuals who played pivotal parts in the ordeal such as the

My Story—Jonathan B Taylor

mysterious hypnotist who seemed to be locked in a mind-bending battle with my birth family to free me from his hold.

My Story—Jonathan B Taylor

Strewn Along the Highway

I first learned of the bodies in 1983 through what would be the vaguest reference. It was sometime during the school year and I was attending junior high in Mattapoisett. One morning, while riding the bus to school my attention was called to a man who was standing on the side of the road along Route 6 at the beginning of a path, which led into the woods. The other children were marveling at the man's appearance. He was an extremely large individual with an exaggerated muscular build whose thick dark hair and beard gave him a slight resemblance to a wolf man. However, my focus was drawn to his strangely piercing blue eyes, which captured me in their gaze. After freezing me in his beckoning stare, he turned and proceeded toward the path that led into the woods.

Later that day, I walked away from the school before my second to last period and headed down Route 6 toward the path that led into the forest. Journeying down that path, I encountered the mysterious figure that I had seen that morning. He was standing by a makeshift tent, which had been fashioned out of a canvas tarp and some rope. My first instinct was to run but after just a few short steps, he called to me and I was stopped dead in my tracks. Exhibiting some kind of hold over me, I followed him into his tent where we sat on folded legs

My Story—Jonathan B Taylor

across from each other and he proceeded to tell me his tale. He told me that he had hypnotized me years before as part of what he described as an elaborate test. His last words that I remember before inky blackness were, "There are going to be bodies".

The next day, I was brought before the school administration regarding my early departure. Having no memory of the event at that time, I was oblivious and dumbfounded by the accusations of me leaving the school early on the previous day. Suddenly, in the middle of the inquisition, without any explanation, the matter was dropped and I was permitted to leave, free from any repercussions for my derelict behavior. However, I recall as I left the room, at least one school official remained outraged over the incident and expressed his discontent before letting the matter go.

I next heard of the bodies in the summer of 1984. It was late at night and I was walking toward the beach after talking with a girl that I knew, when I was surrounded by a group of youths. Seizing my arms, they told me that their friend wanted to talk to me. I thought that I was being jumped and I began to curse at them loudly in the night as I attempted to fight off my perceived attackers. At that moment, David Vermette, the individual for whom they were holding me approached us. He told them to release me and I immediately became relaxed. He then took me for a walk alone down what had

My Story—Jonathan B Taylor

once been a road but was now merely a path through some dense overgrowth. He told me that we were brothers and that our mother had given birth to me when she was fourteen and him when she was thirteen. He said that she had given us up for adoption and that I would encounter her in the near future when I moved to New Bedford, which I was set to do at the end of the summer. He explained that I had been hypnotized as a child to suppress any memories or knowledge of my adoption and he described the man who I had met up with in the woods as the one who was responsible for this.

Finally, he spoke of the bodies. His reference was more detailed than the vague allusion that had been made by the man in the forest. He elaborated that there would be a string of murders that was going to take place in the not too distant future. He said that I would hear about these bodies turning up and when that happened, I would remember our conversation from that night and his telling me about those murders. As we parted, I once again found my mind submerged in a river of blackness.

The next day, the girl with whom I had been talking with asked me about the previous night's events. She had heard the commotion and wanted to know if I knew anything about it. I had no memory of the encounter at that time and therefore, had no idea to what she was referring.

My Story—Jonathan B Taylor

At the end of summer in 1984, I moved to New Bedford and began attending New Bedford High. The school eventually became a mere meeting place where I would hook up with my friends before heading for downtown New Bedford. There we would spend our days exploring the city and experiencing the curriculum offered by its streets. On one of those occasions, I was with two other delinquent teens when the three of us went into city hall to get birth certificates. The clerk who was issuing our birth certificates informed us that one of us was adopted and that our birth mother had us when she was only fourteen years old. Just as had been suggested it would, the memory of this event was immediately lost to me. However, it wasn't lost forever and years later when the memory of the event resurfaced, my two companions from that day corroborated it.

In 1985, while cutting school in the downtown area, I finally had my encounter with the woman who identified herself as my birth mother. I was in the New Bedford Public Library when she confronted me in the stairwell. She had birth records, which had been stolen from some state or local agency, listed her as my mother and indicated that she had been fourteen-years-old at the time of my birth. She also had birth records showing that she had given birth to another son when she was thirteen. For the first time, I found that I was able to retain this information without my knowledge or memory of it being

My Story—Jonathan B Taylor

suppressed. I also found myself overwhelmed by unwarranted feelings of hatred toward her. She explained that these feelings were a side effect of her telling me that she was my mother. This was all due to posthypnotic suggestions that had been placed in my mind by the man who had hypnotized me. When we parted ways, she told me that I was to get myself suspended from school for two weeks and meet up with her again at the New Bedford Public Library and once again, the memory of our encounter and any knowledge of adoption were lost to me.

Although I had no memory of our encounter, I did manage to get myself suspended from school for two weeks as she had suggested and as though operating on some kind of autopilot, I found myself back at the library. As before, she showed me the birth records that she possessed and brought me to the point where I was able to retain the information regarding adoption. And, just as before, I was overwhelmed with uncontrollable feelings of hatred toward her.

Over the next two weeks, she laid out her plans for the future to me, filling my head with the information that she chose to provide. She told me that my being hypnotized was a form of retaliation for her having revealed to me that I was adopted during a meeting between us when I was just five years old. She described the man whom I had encountered in the woods and explained that he had

My Story—Jonathan B Taylor

brainwashed me as a child by using hypnosis. The hypnosis related amnesia that I suffered was a result of my mind being placed in a state where any information regarding adoption would be suppressed and removed from my awareness. However, she was given the power to free me from that state although doing so resulted in feelings of hatred toward her, induced by post hypnotic suggestion.

Then she told me about 'the light people' and this provided a window into what drove and motivated her. To explain the 'light people' requires a brief education on the subject of hypnosis and what happens to people when they are placed in a trance. Where most people when placed under hypnosis will recount memories of past lives, there are some people who tell a different story when placed under hypnosis. They describe themselves as 'beings of pure energy' that travel here from another world. Entering the physical form at birth just as any other soul, they claim to be sent here by 'planners' who in turn answer to 'master planners'. These individuals have come to be referred to by some as the 'light people' and where most souls are here to learn lessons, the light people claim they are here to be tested. It should be noted that, for those who believe in the concept of past lives, the soul is not subject to the laws of the physical world and therefore, all souls are capable of experiencing many lives on many different worlds.

My Story—Jonathan B Taylor

She claimed that she was one of these 'planners' and that the man who had hypnotized me was the 'master planner'. He convinced her that he had set the whole thing up as some kind of test for her. Her task was to free me from the hypnosis without me hating her as a result. She said that nothing in this world mattered except this test and it was clear that she was willing to do anything to succeed. Unfortunately, for my part, recounting tales of brainwashing, followed by stories about 'light people' may only serve to incite skepticism but as integral parts of the plot, there is no way around those disclosures.

Finally, she told me about the bodies. Although she wasn't the first to make reference to the imminent murders, she was the only one who actually claimed to be the future killer. She said that she was going to commit a string of serial murders. All of the victims would be women linked to drugs. Their addictions would make them easily lured and their association with drugs would provide a level of indifference on the part of authorities in solving their murders. She was confident that no one would ever suspect a woman of committing the killings, including the victims themselves. Even if they were aware that women were disappearing, they would feel safe and at ease with her. She also claimed to possess a photographic memory and a black belt in martial arts, which would serve as vital tools in completing her task. There was also a suggestion that the placement

My Story—Jonathan B Taylor

of the bodies would be key. She indicated that they would all be placed in the fetal position. However, it is unclear if this was her true intention or well placed misdirection meant to discredit me as no such information was ever revealed publicly that I am aware of so, only the authorities would know if she actually followed through with that undertaking. She said that as the bodies were being discovered, I would hear about it through the media and as the story ran in the news, it would act as a key to unlock a back door that would trigger the release of my suppressed memories. The man who had hypnotized me planted this key during our encounter in the woods, before providing the information to her. This back door would allow her to reveal herself indirectly to me by granting me access to those hidden memories.

One of those days that we spent together included a meeting with her ex-husband, Paul Pothier, Sr., who identified himself as my father at that time. I was stunned by the uncanny resemblance that he bore to the individual who had claimed that we were brothers back in 1984. This meeting provided at least one certainty in a future sea of doubt. There was no question that my proclaimed brother was the son of these two individuals. Something else significant occurred during that meeting. She grew angry with me when I openly inquired, "Does he know about the bodies?" Apparently, he hadn't known about them, prior to that moment.

My Story—Jonathan B Taylor

As our two weeks together drew to a close, there was one final task, which she needed me to perform. Nestled within the buildings of downtown New Bedford was a small church. It was within that church, where she sent me to enter the confessional and inform the priest of the impending murders. With that final seed planted, our time together was done. However, it wasn't the last that I would see of her and as we went our separate ways, my memory of our time together was washed away with the promise that it would one-day return.

In 1987, I was traveling on the highway from New Bedford to Mattapoisett, when I saw a grey van parked along the shoulder. Standing beside the van was the individual that had identified himself as my brother in 1984 when he had alerted me to the future discovery of the bodies. The van's driver was Ted Carney, a man who would later be named as my alleged brother's unwitting accomplice in a case of attempted murder. A few days later, I saw the grey van on the side of the highway again. Only this time, I saw my proclaimed brother running from the woods to the van in a panic. He had the unmistakable look of someone who had just been caught in the act. He was giving the impression of his involvement in something, which had not yet begun to take place.

My Story—Jonathan B Taylor

As foretold, the bodies began turning up and in the spring of 1989 while the story of a serial killer striking the New Bedford area dominated the news, I found myself overwhelmed by the return of memories that were previously lost to me. All of those haunting images consisted of occasions where my mind had suppressed information regarding adoption. Laced among those recovered recollections, were the chilling images of those three individuals who spoke of impending murders years before they actually occurred. Just as the self-professed killer had calculated, no one ever suspected a woman of committing the crimes. The authorities were locked into a search for a male suspect apparently misdirected by DNA evidence, which indicated that the person they sought was a male. This distressing knowledge accompanied some of the most disturbing memories to trouble me. In those memories, I saw flashes of myself walking out of my residence in the north end of New Bedford subsequent to some personal recreation. Walking into the night, I curiously found myself at the head of a path that led into the woods where I carelessly discarded the remnants of the evening's aforementioned activities. On at least one of those occasions, I heard the voice of someone on the path whisper to me from the darkness. I asked who was there but there was no answer.

The memories of mindlessly casting DNA samples into the woods and the mysterious voice in the night weighed heavily on my

My Story—Jonathan B Taylor

thoughts in 2000 when as a prisoner, they collected my DNA to enter into a database for comparison with unsolved crimes. My concerns intensified when after the approximate one month that it would take to process my DNA and enter it into their database, authorities announced that they were reopening the investigation into the New Bedford Highway Killings. I wondered; was the voice in the night, the voice of an unseen killer who lurked in the shadows, acquiring my DNA to dapple on their crime scene canvas? Although those fears plagued me for a time, the passage of time would eventually lay them to rest.

Now, after decades of silence and a journey that has led me down virtually every path of an insolvable maze, I find myself standing at the threshold of the only remaining path left to travel. It is the path of revelation. Pulling its rusty gate free from overgrowth's relentless grip, I begin the long walk into the unknown by laying my cards on the table and my soul bare. As I traveled through my life, individuals planted the seeds of revelations regarding murders set to take place in a future of their own design. They planted those seeds in suppressed memories with the knowledge that one day those memories would resurface. These are things that I would never have revealed, were it not presumably the will of those who made the revelations as they continue to test authority's resolve to keep its own secrets safe.

My Story—Jonathan B Taylor

The Back Story:

It all began with a broken promise and a lie, which sent the situation into a slow, deliberate spin that would eventually spiral out of control. On the day that I was born, my fourteen-year-old birth mother gave me to a couple who was in the same hospital after suffering a miscarriage. Her only request was that they promise to raise me with the knowledge that I was adopted. They gave her their word and she gave them her son.

Unfortunately, their word was never kept. Instead, they chose to conceal my adoption from me with the claim that they would reveal the truth when I was sixteen. The first flaw in their plan appeared when I was five and a neighbor named Barbara King let it slip that I was adopted. This wasn't the first time that the subject had come up but it was the first time that I actually had some proof. Outraged over being lied to, this led to an angry confrontation between me and my adoptive parents who quelled the situation with denials and lies but the distrust and animosity remained and now they had seen a preview of how I would react to the truth if it ever were revealed.

A solution was presented by a mysterious figure who had befriended them. A psychologist specializing in hypnosis, he explained that the memory of my neighbor's revelation could be suppressed through hypnosis as though it had never occurred. It was determined that the current situation didn't justify such extreme measures but a tempting seed had been planted.

Later that year, the circumstances changed when I was brought to a small pond where my birth mother could often be found on a Sunday morning fishing with my birth father and her one-year-old son, Paul Pothier, Jr.. This was where the truth finally came to light. When I approached them, she introduced me to my younger brother and identified herself as my birth mother. With those words, the plunger was pressed and the scene exploded. In a sudden change of strategy, my adoptive parents who had always denied that I was adopted chose this moment to admit it and for the first time, I knew it was true because I was hearing it from them.

They lashed out at my birth mother for revealing the truth, while I lashed out at them for lying. My birth mother was under the impression that I knew about my adoption and she reminded them of their promise to raise me with that knowledge. They fired back by announcing their intention to tell me when I was sixteen and stated with a sense of victory that regardless of any promise, she had no right to tell me.

My Story—Jonathan B Taylor

The next thing I knew, I was extracted from the scene and thrown in the back seat of the car where I continued to curse them and demand to be returned to my birth family. As we drove away, it appeared that things could not have gone worse for my adoptive parents when in fact, they could not have gone better. Now they had the perfect scenario to justify their diabolical plans, which I heard them discussing as we headed down the road. What would seem like a lightning strike response to an unexpected development was actually months in the making.

That week, I shared my tale with my friend at school while some of the other wide-eyed children listened intently. As I recounted my adventure, I explained how my birth mother was only fourteen when she had me and rationalized that now, she was old enough for me to be returned to her. I was unaware that it was socially unacceptable for adopted children to feel this way or of the lengths that people would go to in order to stop it.

Focused on reuniting with my birth family, I determined that there was only one thing that stood in the way. My adoptive parents showed no intentions of relinquishing me. If the problem was that they wanted to keep me, then I needed them to want to get rid of me. I set out to accomplish this through a barrage of venomous language and vicious insults intended to make them despise me to the point that

My Story—Jonathan B Taylor

unloading me back onto my birth mother would become an attractive alternative to keeping me around. This was cruel and insensitive but it was child's play compared to what they were planning for me. Although I was successful in getting them to despise me, the plan backfired and rather than get rid of the monster that I now presented to them, they instead sought to destroy it.

A trap was set, baited with the thing that I wanted most at that moment. My adoptive parents finally agreed to return me to my birth family but explained that first we had to find them so we were going to see a man who specialized in such tasks. This was my introduction to the mysterious figure who had been skillfully manipulating things as he slid us around like chess pieces on a checkered board. Posing as someone who specialized in finding people, this man who normally donned the cloak of a psychologist, was actually nothing but a hypnotist and his specialty was mind control.

Blinded by my excitement over the prospect of being reunited with my birth family, I trusted my adoptive parents despite their history of lies and followed them foolishly toward a trap door behind, which a spider was waiting. There would be no reunion with my birth family. What they had in store was an unimaginable act of betrayal and the ultimate act of revenge. When the dust settled, the little monster that I created who demanded to be returned to his birth family, would be replaced by a monster of their own making. Through a psychological lobotomy, I would become a mindless zombie in a cage and they would become my captors.

When we entered his office, I was amazed by his remarkable appearance. Although he was playing the part of a locator of lost individuals, he looked the part of a hypnotist. He was a hulking figure with deceptively angelic features that were shrouded in a head of thick, dark, curly hair and beard, emblazoned by a wisp of white that shot from his widow's peak and large, icy blue eyes that froze you in their gaze and, like my birth mother and two brothers, he also possessed the extraordinary gift of a photographic memory.

As a master of his craft, the task was relatively easy. Having no idea what hypnosis was and focused on finding my birth family, I followed his instructions to relax as my eyelids became heavy and the sound of his voice grew hollow and dim. Slipping from consciousness, I floated helplessly into a deep oblivion and with a snap of his fingers, I was gone.

With my mind in a trance, the Svengali chess master was in complete control of my thoughts and free to wield commands in the form of posthypnotic suggestions that I was compelled to follow. First, he instructed me that when I awoke, I would have no knowledge

My Story—Jonathan B Taylor

of being adopted and no memory of any event that concerned my adoption. That information and those memories would remain buried in my subconscious just out of reach, like deleted scenes from a video that could no longer be accessed but stayed etched somewhere on the computer's hard drive.

Additionally, any future information that I was to see or hear, which related to my adoption would be automatically suppressed as well. Now, if anyone tried to tell me that I was adopted, I would be unable to retain the information and it would be forgotten the moment that my mind processed it. He also included a provision wherein I would be overwhelmed with uncontrollable feelings of hatred and anger directed toward any person who revealed that I was adopted, forcing me to lash out at them with expressions of false loathing before the memory of the entire event was suppressed and buried in my subconscious. This was retaliation for telling my adoptive parents that I hated them for lying about my adoption. It allowed them to turn the tables so that I would now be saying those words to anyone who tried to tell me the truth.

Next, he instructed me to move my eyes all the way to the right, then all the way to the left, and then straight up and down, forming the shape of an iron cross. From that point on, anytime that I was confronted with information that concerned my adoption, my eyes

My Story—Jonathan B Taylor

would flash through this sequence repeatedly as the memory of the event was being suppressed. This simulated the rapid eye movement that is experienced during states of deep sleep and would brand the suppressed memories of actual events with the impressions of those that occurred in my dreams, making it difficult to distinguish between the two.

In keeping with the revenge theme, I was shown a mirror and instructed to see a warped and distorted reflection. This was the face, which would stare back at me in any future images that I saw of myself. What amounted to mental disfigurement was further payback for the insults of my campaign to make them despise me. It was the psychological equivalent to pouring acid over my head and served no tactical purpose.

With these posthypnotic suggestions in play, people who knew about my adoption no longer had the ability to reveal that information to me. Any mention of my adoption would be met with the spectacle of my eyes flashing through their dizzying sequence, followed by my declarations of hatred toward the person and finally my suppression of the memory as though it had never occurred. This provided a source of amusement to some sadistic individuals who would openly discuss my adoption in front of me to witness the display, creating hundreds of suppressed memories for my subconscious video library.

My Story—Jonathan B Taylor

Because this was being done to me against my will, it meant that my true self with all of my genuine feelings and memories was imprisoned somewhere in the back of my mind, struggling to break free. This inner conflict could lead to uprisings by my subconscious in, which my suppressed memories would begin to resurface. If I were to reach this state of awareness, my mind would no longer block out information related to my adoption, making me receptive to the truth.

In order to get me back in my cage, my antagonists would have to lure me into a prearranged situation that involved a ritual of images and phrases designed to reinforce my brainwashing by way of posthypnotic suggestion. These visions and incantations had the power to return me to that state of oblivion where my mind would instantly suppress information related to my adoption. To spring this trap, they would need me to remain in a state of uncertainty about my adoption. Disguising my resurfaced memories as dreams was a clever tactic that would certainly keep me guessing but my nemesis required the cooperation of those who knew the truth in order to subdue me in complete disbelief. Suddenly, they had the ability to reveal information to me about my adoption without my mind suppressing it so he needed to ensure that they didn't. If they refused to remain silent or perpetuate the lie then they could end up blowing the whole caper.

My Story—Jonathan B Taylor

The key to making these minions abandon their morals was providing them with a means to justify their wicked actions. This was accomplished masterfully by shifting responsibility for what was being done to me onto my birth mother. The perpetrators made the case that it was her actions that forced them to take such extreme measures. They further elaborated that she was given the ability to free me from my hypnotic prison and therefore could end it at any time although my brainwashing would cause me to hate her as a result. By casting her as the source of my suffering and the reason that it was allowed to continue, she provided an imaginary blanket of justification to spread out over all the participants, absolving them of their own guilt-ridden roles. The hypnotist would then take it a step further by eventually forcing my birth mother into a pattern of abandoning all of her children in an effort to make her appear as an even less sympathetic figure so that in order to save one child, she would have to sacrifice her relationship with the others.

What started out as just a lie, had become something far worse and unimaginable. Taking on a life of its own, the juggernaut would swallow everyone in its path, turning decent, honest people into cheap, worthless liars. But, anything that is based on a lie has a flaw in its foundation. All lies are threatened by the truth and like a crack, as the lie grows, it produces greater weakness in the structure, making the pressure provided by the truth ever more powerful.

My Story—Jonathan B Taylor

The ability to bend others to his will when there was nothing in it for them was perhaps the greatest trick that the magician would pull from his sleeve. It was inconceivable to think that anyone would go along with something so immoral when they would never be okay with it being done to them but somehow they saw past their consciences and became twisted servants to an evil master.

Although it was being sold as an act of retaliation against my birth mother for revealing the truth about my adoption, the main objective of the nefarious plot was restoration and preservation of the lie. Following their latest exploits, my captors' obsession with keeping the truth from me had taken on a whole new meaning. There was no way they could let me find out what they had done now so they needed to take some extra steps to cover their tracks. Since the threat of me hating her was the only thing that stood in the way of my birth mother revealing the truth and breaking my chains, the puppet master provided some added precautions to keep her in check and prevent her from taking down the house of cards.

When it came to mind games, he was the king and he had something special in store for her. It involved an unusual phenomenon in, which certain people under hypnosis will claim to be traveling entities from another world that were sent here by 'planners' who in turn answer to 'master planners'. His intention was to tell my birth mother that I had revealed myself to be one of these individuals while I was in a trance and that I had identified her as one of the 'planners'.

That set the stage for his next move, which was to present her with a perplexing predicament that was right out of this world. He would spring it on her that he was actually a 'master planner' and explain that he had created this situation as an elaborate test. Her task was to free me from the hypnosis without me hating her as a result. For that to happen, she would need me to learn the truth about my adoption but it couldn't come from her or from anyone that she told. Nor could it be traced back to anything that she did. As farfetched as it was, with the possibility of this actually being a test looming and the uncertainty of the consequences for failure, it seemed like the smart move was to play by his rules.

Having her hands tied by impossible parameters meant that she could only bring me out of it so far and the rest was up to me. I had to find the truth out for myself so she would have to take me to a place where I could begin to look for it. To get me there, she would need to trigger the release of my suppressed memories. This would bring me to that level of awareness where my mind was no longer suppressing information about my adoption and I could actively seek the truth.

My Story—Jonathan B Taylor

Once she accomplished this, I would be on my own. She would be forced to turn on me and I would have to find my way through the maze alone, avoiding the perilous traps that threatened to launch me back to oblivion. In my quest for the truth, I would find myself pitted against my birth mother whose new task would be to close the door on all roads leading back to her. She would be working against me now to ensure that I didn't learn the truth from anyone that she told or because of anything that she did.

My hope was hanging on the hearts of those individuals who had learned the truth about my adoption through my captors and my fate was resting in their hands. Two armies had emerged on the battlefield. There were those who sought to subdue me in the clutches of evil and those who fought to free me from them. Some were forced to lie by the rules of the game while others lied by choice. In order to end the horror show, I needed the members of the wind-up infantry who fought and lied for my captors to have a change of heart. If they could snap out of their own trances, then there was a chance that they might abandon treachery and deceit for a final rally with truth and honesty, redeeming themselves in the process by rescuing me from their own attack and applying tourniquets to wounds, which they had inflicted.

It seemed unlikely that my captors' accomplices would suddenly want to save me after working so hard toward my destruction but not

My Story—Jonathan B Taylor

all hope was lost. Beyond the bleakness and amidst the shadows, there was a small group of rebels who had crept across the lines and slipped past the sentries. These forgotten warriors were unique because they had learned the truth about my adoption from me. They were the children at school with whom I had shared my tale and witnessed my transformation into the soulless zombie with spastic eyes. There was a provision that applied to my one friend but left the others unaccounted. Because they hadn't learned of my adoption from my birth mother, there was nothing in the parameters to prevent them from revealing what they knew. The only provision was that their decision to reveal the truth couldn't be influenced by her. I couldn't force anyone to speak out but if they were able to find it in their own hearts to come forward or if I could somehow persuade them with my words, then they could be the key to unlocking everything, including my cage. Armed with the truth, these unstoppable soldiers could take down anyone or anything that stood in their way. For, the mere threat of exposure could be enough to force the powers that be to release me from their hold. This theory may have already been demonstrated once in a Wareham District Court room.

My Story—Jonathan B Taylor

May 14, 1993

In May of 1993, I was working as a long distance truck driver and would frequently find myself in precarious places at all hours of the night where danger often lurked in the darkness. As I crisscrossed the country and heard truck stop tales of drivers being robbed and killed, I began to arm myself accordingly. I first acquired a knife then, a stun gun and eventually a crossbow. I kept these weapons in a black canvas duffle bag including the crossbow, which could be easily broken down for compact storage. I was aware that crossbows and stun guns were illegal in certain states and the potential risks of possessing such items would play a pivotal part in things to come.

On May 14, 1993, I was taking a break from my perpetual road trip around the country on a stop over in Southeastern Massachusetts. While in the area, I would usually find a couch to crash on and this night I had landed on the couch of my childhood home on Channel Street in the Crescent Beach area of Mattapoisett. I was due to head back out on the road in the morning and hoped to get some sleep before I left. Unfortunately, because of my odd work hours and sporadic sleep schedule as a trucker, slumber sometimes eluded me and in the predawn hours, I found myself awake and standing outside on the front porch smoking a cigarette.

My Story—Jonathan B Taylor

Earlier I had heard the sound of something scratching on the side of the house and I walked around to investigate when I noticed a skunk lumbering through the neighbor's backyard. In the first of a series of bad moves, I went to my car and retrieved the black canvas duffle bag from the trunk, which contained my knife, stun gun and crossbow, along with some other items including a flashlight, some arrows and a walkman style stereo cassette player. I assembled the crossbow and went to the backyard where I fired a wild shot at the skunk before it disappeared into some brush that separated the neighbor's backyard from the yard behind it. The Crescent Beach area was a grid of dirt roads accessible by a paved main road, which ran through it. Most of the houses in the area consisted of seasonal homes that were empty during that time of year so I was able to walk at liberty through the open yards looking for the lost skunk.

At some point, I spotted a fox, which became the new target of my pursuit. The fox kept a safe distance but didn't flee into the woods. It wandered through yards, allowing me to stay with it for the most part and eventually luring me down the main road to a marshy area with a small creek carved through the middle of it. I don't know what drove me to pursue a skunk or a fox in the dark of the night but I had previously only shot my crossbow at stationary targets and this was my first attempt at using it in a hunting type situation. With crossbows being illegal in Massachusetts, there was actually less risk in carrying

My Story—Jonathan B Taylor

one at night as opposed to walking around with it in broad daylight. However, there was always the risk of encountering a patrolling police cruiser so I mostly kept to the shadows and stayed out of sight.

Eventually, my pursuit of the fox ended and it was time to head back. In the distance, I heard a loud noise that sounded like a balloon popping. I next heard the sound of a gunning motor accompanied by tires spinning on gravel and screeching loudly as they met the pavement. The commotion seemed to come from the Channel Street area and as the accelerating engine trailed off in the distance, I thought that someone had hit something with their car and was fleeing the scene of an accident.

When I reached the house, I discovered that it was on fire. It was still dark out and an orange glow had filled the night sky. Approaching through the backyard, I panicked and ran back and forth trying to decide what to do when a window blew out and flames erupted. I saw the two propane tanks on the back of the house and realized they could explode so I retreated to the neighboring yard behind the house. At this point, I could hear fire engines approaching in the distance and saw the distinctive flashing blue light of a police car lighting up the sky, allowing me to track its movements as it came down the road and turned onto Channel Street.

My Story—Jonathan B Taylor

Suddenly, the police car's presence reminded me that I still had my canvas duffel bag containing an illegal stun gun strapped across my shoulder. I knew that I had to get rid of it so, I ran across the street to ditch it in the woods. By the time I reached my destination, I realized that I was missing something. In the commotion, I had dropped my crossbow and it was too late to go back for it. The dreaded scenario of being arrested and fired from my job, which had played out in my head since acquiring the crossbow was now becoming a reality. Although the discovery of the fire was deeply concerning, my thoughts were consumed by the dilemma of the crossbow and how to get out of that predicament. As I tried to resolve it in my mind, I continued walking deeper into the woods, putting further distance between myself and the unraveling situation.

After a period of walking aimlessly through the woods, I became fatigued. I hadn't really slept in the past forty-eight hours and was being relentlessly attacked by mosquitoes. I still didn't know the seriousness of the fire but when I heard helicopters overhead, I thought that it was a bad sign. I had discarded my knife and stun gun in a small pond but still had my walkman radio in my duffel bag and learned through news accounts that there were fatalities. My concerns about the crossbow suddenly became irrelevant. I stopped at the site of my 1983 encounter with the man who claimed to have hypnotized me and spoke of the impending 'bodies'. The canvas tarp from his makeshift tent lay buried under a blanket of pine needles right where he had left it. I placed my duffel bag under the tarp and as I proceeded to make my way out of the woods, I thought about everything that he had done to me and wondered how this latest turn of events fit into his twisted master plan? In the evil game of cat and mouse between my birth mother and the hypnotist, she had been tasked with finding a way out of his mind-bending challenge for us and I was sure that whatever was happening had to do with those efforts. Unfortunately, my foolish faith in her ability to resolve things would contribute to my downfall.

While working my way back to the scene of the fire, I encountered State Police Detective Scott Berna and an Officer Glasheen on the path. After an initially tense moment in, which I was pat frisked, I identified myself and they said that I was the person they were looking for. I told them that I expected to see them, having heard the news reports of the fire on the radio. They asked where my radio was and whether I had brought anything else with me into the woods. I led them to the duffel bag, which contained my walkman radio and then showed them the small pond where I had discarded my knife and stun gun. During this time, they attempted to question me about the fire. I didn't know anything about the fire other than what I had heard and seen but was intending to come clean about my illicit activities with the crossbow. At that point, I just wanted to get out of the woods

My Story—Jonathan B Taylor

so I told them that I would talk to them but that I didn't want to do it there. It was then decided that they would take me to the police station for questioning.

As we walked through the woods, they continued to pepper me with questions. They said that they needed to know what happened back at the house. I told them that they knew what happened. There was a fire and the house burned down. They said that they understood that but needed to know why the fire happened and asked me if I was responsible for setting it. I just kept shaking my head, 'No.' and the more I became aware of what they were accusing me, the less I felt like talking to them. We exited the woods to a waiting police car that drove us to the station. When we arrived, I was given a paper to sign, which informed me of my rights during questioning. I told them that I would answer their questions but that I wanted to exercise my right to have an attorney present. This didn't sit well with them and while I was working to obtain an attorney through the Committee for Public Counsel Services, they were obtaining warrants to seize my clothing and search my car.

I never got a chance to give my statement. When my attorney, Joseph Krowski, Sr. arrived, he shut down the interrogation. He explained to me that the District Attorney had declared that the fire was arson and they had zeroed in on me as their suspect. He said that they were coming for me and it was his job to defend me. He made me assure him that I would not discuss the case with anyone and after surrendering my clothing to police, I was free to leave while the devious authorities went to work framing a case against me.

The deceptions began when the two detectives that I encountered in the woods sat down together several hours afterward and crafted an account of our meeting. [Trial transcript pgs. 5-136 thru 5-137: During cross-examination, Trooper Scott Berna admits to sitting down with Trooper Glasheen and collaborating on their reports.] Instead of sitting down separately and recounting their individual recollections while writing their own reports, these two collaborated on their statement to avoid any inconsistencies. This tactic allowed them to use their imaginations and make certain omissions without contradicting each other. Detectives routinely engage in these creative writing exercises in order to conceal violations of a suspect's rights or to bolster their case against someone they believe to be guilty. However, when people fabricate facts, they often make mistakes and leave holes in their stories. In this case, the deceitful detectives showed their hand when they wrote in the initial affidavit for the search warrant applications, 'When confronted, the suspect made the statements, "I know why you're here." and "You already know what happened."' Later while constructing their joint report, they added, 'When asked why he didn't run, the suspect responded, "It's no fun hiding.'" This was a lie, which actually referenced a comment that one of the detectives had made. He had asked me why I didn't run and when I didn't respond, He said, "I guess it's no fun hiding. Huh?" The fact that there was no mention of the far more problematic statement in the earlier applications for the warrants exposes its origins. Such an ominous reply would have been the lead statement in their affidavit and not a mere afterthought in the subsequent report.

Three days later, I was arrested and charged with arson and murder after hypersensitive testing revealed microscopic traces of a petroleum based product on my sneakers. As a truck driver who pumped my own gas and fuel, it would be surprising if I didn't have traces of petroleum on my footwear. Anyone who uses a self-service fueling station will likely pick up traces of petroleum on their shoes through simple contact with the surface around a fuel pump and will inadvertently have drops of petroleum land on their footwear when removing the nozzle from the vehicle after fueling. As oil based products, those substances will linger.

In other results of their investigation, authorities said they found the melted remnants of a red plastic gas can in the debris around the front entryway of the house. Additionally, first responders described seeing an oily sheen on the water after the fire was extinguished and wood samples taken from scent dog alerts on the foyer and stairs

My Story—Jonathan B Taylor

leading up to the second floor, tested positive for traces of petroleum. However, a retired firefighter that lived across the street described seeing a gas can like the one that was found being stored in that general area in a nook beside a large wood box on the front porch in the days leading up to the fire. Another firefighter who was active at the scene, reported entering the structure and making his way up the stairs, which would have led him right through the water with the oily sheen, contaminating the alleged crime scene by tracking trace evidence along his path.

Following my arrest, one detective found his way to the local service station to inquire if anyone had purchased gas in a red container during the previous week. This fishing expedition produced some of the most puzzling and frustrating evidence against me. A clerk named Glenn LeBlanc reported that someone fitting my description had come into the station on May 13 and attempted to purchase gas in a milk jug. The clerk told the customer that he could not sell him gas in a plastic milk jug and when the man asked, "Why?" the clerk explained that it was illegal. After arguing briefly and insisting that he 'needed the gas', the patron was allowed to purchase gas in a government approved red plastic container. The clerk also claimed that the customer was unable to operate the self-service pump and required assistance. After overfilling the container, he loaded the gasoline soaked item into his vehicle, which was parked around the

My Story—Jonathan B Taylor

corner. The clerk was shown a photo array from, which he identified my picture as the person who purchased gas that day.

Having worked at a gas station, I am fully aware that you cannot put gas in a plastic milk jug and would never attempt to do so. I was also completely capable of operating a gas pump without requiring assistance and could have easily retrieved gasoline from the tank on my car if I needed it so badly. I would have accepted this as a case of mistaken identity but I was troubled by some of the more questionable assertions made by the clerk. He claimed that he didn't know who I was and had never seen me before, despite having both grown up in the same small town and crossing paths thousands of times. He also denied seeing any news coverage of the fire or my arrest and insisted that he didn't discuss the case with anyone prior to picking my photo out of the lineup. His convenient answers made his involvement feel somewhat staged. Admitting to those things would have called his whole story into question. If he knew who I was and was aware of the fire, he would have come forward with his claims immediately and not had to identify me from a photo array. He also claimed to remember all of these details about the encounter but couldn't remember anything about what the person was wearing.

By injecting himself into the case, he was able to ingratiate himself with authorities who reportedly let him off the hook when

My Story—Jonathan B Taylor

they discovered him one night with teenaged boys and alcohol behind the town middle school. Eventually, his bad behavior caught up with him and he pled guilty to child molestation charges a couple of years later.

Questionable identifications aside, it was a deeply disturbing coincidence to have someone fitting my general description make such a spectacle of himself while purchasing gas at a local service station the day before I'm accused of setting a fatal fire. The description of his vehicle was even similar to mine except that his was described as being covered in patches of rust, which mine was not. Another factor showed it was not my vehicle. The person who purchased gas had overfilled the container and placed it in their car. However, the authorities had their canine go through my entire car and found no traces of an accelerant on any part of the interior.

This absurd accusation also created one of the biggest inconsistencies in the Commonwealth's case against me. We know that a melted plastic gas container was found in the debris in the area of the front porch. We also know that William King, a retired Firefighter who lived across the street, reported seeing a red plastic container of gasoline being stored in that same area on the previous day, May 13, 1993. (Trial transcript pgs. 6-13 through 6-15) This fact was also corroborated by another witness who told Trooper Joseph

My Story—Jonathan B Taylor

Mason in his 5/27/93 report that gasoline was being stored in a red plastic container on the front porch. However, the problem with the Commonwealth's case is that only one gas can was found in the debris and since that can has already been accounted for, where is this other can that I'm supposed to have caused a big seen over at the local Mobil Station the day before? Unfortunately, this discrepancy was never pointed out at trial and didn't occur to me until years later.

As the nightmare unfolded, I was brought before a Wareham District Court Judge and held without bail after prosecutors provided a preliminary presentation of their case against me. They laid out an impossible scenario, which had me pouring over two gallons of gasoline down a darkened stairway at night without splashing any of it on my clothing except for microscopic traces on my sneakers. They then hypothesized that I somehow ignited this volatile pool although they provided no explanation for how I could have done so without being severely injured by the resulting fireball that would be sure to follow. They also implied that there was something sinister about a bag of clothes that was in my car, knowing that I was scheduled to leave on a road trip that morning. There was another item in my car that would play a much larger part in their case. Police seized a soft leather briefcase from the trunk of my car, containing written materials and recordings related to a book that I had written, which was based on my experience with resurfaced memories regarding adoption and hypnosis. I had been directed to write this book by my birth mother years earlier, unaware that I was creating evidence to be used against me in a future frame up.

In the dirtiest move imaginable, authorities revealed their intentions to deliver the ultimate act of deception. They would misuse my book by distorting it with a false narrative in order to portray it as evidence of a motive. Prosecutors claimed that the fire was an act of retaliation for what they characterized as an incorrect belief that I was adopted and had been hypnotized as a child to conceal the information from me. The problem with this approach was that they were knowingly basing their entire case on a lie. It was a brazen move considering the number of people who knew the truth about my childhood brainwashing and could easily call them on it. I was sure that there was no way that every one of those potential witnesses would allow the authorities to proceed with such a plot.

My confidence in those potential plot spoilers was confirmed in a phone call with my attorney following that initial court appearance. Speaking to him from a jail cell, my attorney informed me that people were beginning to 'come forward'. I asked him who the people were and he mentioned some names such as King, Mahady, and Keough who were all Crescent Beach residents that I knew to have firsthand knowledge of my adoption and hypnosis. He didn't want to discuss

My Story—Jonathan B Taylor

what was said to him over the phone but assured me that he was aware of the truth about my situation and would be coming to speak with me in person.

A few weeks later, my attorney visited me in lockup and I pressed him for the specifics of what he had learned from those individuals that had 'come forward'. He said that before he would divulge any details of their revelations, he needed to know if I was responsible for setting the fire. When I told him that I was not, he refused to elaborate further on what was revealed to him. I was troubled by the fact that he was withholding information from me and pointed out that his unusual ultimatum would call any resulting confession into obvious question. Although he kept quiet on the comments of those who came forward, he did tell me that he tracked down my alleged birth mother, Mary Beth Vickers, and learned from her mother that she was seeing a psychiatrist because she believed that she had been hypnotized as a teenager to suppress her memory of giving up two children for adoption. I didn't know what her game was but I told him that she wasn't going to help us and he responded by insisting that she was.

Several weeks after that, my attorney filed a motion in the Wareham District Court to have the case dismissed and the judge allowed it. I walked out of the courthouse free from all charges only to be rearrested a few hours later and brought before the same judge

My Story—Jonathan B Taylor

the next day who lambasted the prosecutor for not challenging his ruling through proper appeals proceedings. He released me again from his court only, this time on personal recognizance and issued an order barring authorities from arresting me a third time. This prompted the prosecutor to railroad an indictment against me and after voluntarily appearing in the Brockton Superior Court, I was granted a low bail of $15,000 and spent the next two years awaiting trial on the street. There were some indications that this startling turn of events was the result of the Commonwealth's reluctance to produce discovery documents related to my adoption and hypnosis in court, which allowed the judge to grant the extraordinary relief.

My attorney's success at having the case dismissed and securing my new found freedom lulled me into a false sense of security, compounded by a blind faith in his abilities, which would ultimately come back to haunt me. Behind the scenes and beyond the event horizon, pressure was mounting on my attorney to turn on me. The first warning signs of his imminent defection appeared immediately after my release when he bunkered in his office in response to a barrage of angry phone calls from members of the Commonwealth, which he likened to having opened a hornet's nest. I was unaware of the influence that the Commonwealth wielded over a public defender, dependant on highly prized appointments to murder trials and unwittingly watched as their pressure campaign put him in check and ensured his cooperation with their ongoing charade.

The false sense of security blanket was snugged even tighter around my neck by conversations with some of the witnesses who had 'come forward' with information following my arrest. When I was finally able to speak with them, two of the individuals apologized for their roles in what had been done to me and confirmed that my attorney was made aware of the truth about my adoption and hypnosis. I was given assurances that they would testify to those facts in court and expose the authorities' misrepresentation of the circumstances surrounding my childhood brainwashing. Unfortunately, there was an undercurrent of culpability that appeared when one of them told me how another individual expressed a fear that the authorities would arrest everyone who knew the truth as accomplices to mind control and murder. Meanwhile, the shadowy figure who had led them down this dark path remained noticeably absent. Nobody seemed to know what happened to the mysterious hypnotist who had orchestrated the evil that was unleashed on me. With a swirl of his cape, he had vanished along with his entire existence. Since there were no public attempts to locate or even acknowledge him, it was the ultimate disappearing act, worthy of his 'master planner' persona.

My Story—Jonathan B Taylor

Despite being long gone, my nemesis' grip on the situation remained strong and was clearly visible at my trial where prosecutors laid out their case against me in the alternate reality, which he had created. Although they were fully aware of the truth regarding my adoption and hypnosis, authorities perjured themselves in open court by misrepresenting those facts as figments of my imagination. It was a new low even for these bottom feeders, which went way beyond moral or ethical violations and crossed the line to being criminal. The fact that the prosecution didn't want the jury to hear the truth about the elusive hypnotist who seized control of my mind when I was five or how he had suddenly disappeared at the same time that the fire occurred was evidence of their own doubts regarding my guilt. If they felt that this information could cause a jury to question my responsibility for the alleged crime, then they had already deemed it worthy of such deduction in their own minds.

The Commonwealth could never have carried out their underhanded actions without the quiet cooperation of the countless witnesses who had firsthand knowledge of my childhood brainwashing and the power to expose the truth at any time. Their silence was crucial to the ruse and while most made their contributions by remaining in the shadows, a handful of henchmen rallied behind the prosecutor and rather than take a stand against him, they took to the stand for him and testified against me. I was left to rely on the empty assurances of some not so former foes that were unfortunately destined to double cross me.

The sadistic game in, which participants attempt to convince someone that he is losing his mind when in fact, they have stolen it, had taken a terrible turn with the target of this treachery on trial for murder. Those left holding the ball by their lost leader were doubling down on the madness and digging themselves in deeper when they should have been bailing. They seemed hell bent on playing this evil contest out to the end and achieving the ultimate goal of my total destruction.

Amidst the barrage of betrayal, there was no greater traitor than my own backstabbing attorney who allowed the prosecution's deceptive tactics despite having both the ability and an obligation to stop them. He even allowed Mr. Dawley to stipulate in open court that my birth mother never had any children when she was thirteen or fourteen in response to a discovery motion that he filed for her medical records, knowing that the prosecutor was perjuring himself. Through his unprecedented cooperation, the opposition was able to introduce hand picked witnesses and written materials, which presented proof of my personal revelations regarding adoption and hypnosis while avoiding any evidence that substantiated those unusual circumstances to be true. Instead of calling them out on the

My Story—Jonathan B Taylor

deception and revealing the truth about my childhood hypnotizing, my complacent attorney stuck to the prosecution's deceitful script and played out his case under the same false narrative with some embellishments of his own. He basically conceded that there was no validity to my adoption and hypnosis by giving the fraudulent impression that those were merely misguided notions from years earlier, which I no longer believed to be true. In painting this false picture of the facts, he was putting words in my mouth while I sat in silence and appeared to endorse those lies.

In a trial full of fabrications, it was inevitable that some of those swirling falsehoods would be attributed to me. Although I sat silent while being buried beneath the pile of lies, I had no intention of remaining that way and planned to crawl my way out by taking the stand when the time came and revealing the truth about the extraordinary circumstances that surrounded my situation.

There were too many unanswered questions and false allegations for me not to take the stand. I had to explain the events that led to my encounter with detectives in the woods. Although I could explain what I was doing, I couldn't answer why I was walking around with a crossbow chasing shadows in the night when the house I had been in ended up on fire. The trouble with being brainwashed is that you wind up doing and saying things, which are beyond your control and can only be explained by the one who cast the spell.

I also had to respond to the outlandish allegation that I stumbled into the local service station the day before the fire and caused a scene while making a bungling attempt to purchase gas in a plastic milk jug. It was too much of a coincidence for someone fitting my description to have randomly incriminated me in such a way. In my experience, nothing happened by chance and every painstaking occurrence went down exactly according to the diabolical plans of a man who had an unusual knack for making people and things go his way.

One of his primary chess pieces was my birth mother who served as the queen and played a critical role in my conviction through her treacherous contributions to the falsified and circumstantial evidence that was stacked against me. She led me to create a trail of written materials and conversations related to my adoption and hypnosis that were deceptively used to incriminate me. However, it was her brazen false statements and testimony, which openly revealed her goal of getting me convicted and demonstrated a direct involvement in my undoing. If she wanted to incriminate me further she could have orchestrated the conspicuous gasoline purchase by sending someone who resembled me to cause a scene at the station that day.

My Story—Jonathan B Taylor

My birth mother's belief that she was being tested by the self-proclaimed 'master planner' who hypnotized me, meant that he called the shots and it was his will that I be condemned for the crimes, which I was accused. While setting me up on murder charges did not seem very sporting, it certainly wasn't surprising considering everything else that had been done to me. Seeing me sentenced to a slow, methodical death by incarceration was just the natural culmination of the evil that was unleashed on me when I was five years old.

For the hypnotist, it was never really about what he could do to me or how much I could endure. The challenge was in seeing how far he could take it and how many rats would be willing to follow. With each line they crossed, the participants journeyed further down the dark path of an illusive ghoul who fed greedily on the souls of those he enslaved.

Unfortunately, my plan to take the stand was sidelined by a perfect storm of deception and the truth never made it to trial. The effort to prevent me from telling my side of the story was led by my attorney who was determined to keep the prosecution's false narrative in play. His insistence that I not testify was coordinated with a campaign of empty assurances meant to muzzle me.

My Story—Jonathan B Taylor

He promised a parade of witnesses, which would include an arson investigator who determined the cause of fire to be accidental, followed by a private investigator who would testify to contradictory statements made by the gas station attendant and finally, my former boss from the service station where I once worked to refute the suggestion that I would be foolish enough to attempt purchasing gasoline in a plastic milk jug. He argued that his array of witnesses would make it unnecessary for me to take the stand and he kept his claims to call these people going right up until the end when he abruptly rested his case without summoning a single one of them to testify.

While my attorney attempted to deter me from testifying with false promises of intended defense witnesses, another factor weighed into the equation. I was in the precarious position of having to prove the truth about my adoption and hypnosis with only my words, against a backdrop of lies that were laid out by the prosecutor and affirmed by my own attorney. Although there were countless individuals who could have backed me up, none of them showed any interest in helping me. Even those who had privately revealed the truth were reluctant to do so publicly.

Although I couldn't physically produce anyone at trial to verify that they knew the truth about my adoption and hypnosis, I did have evidence to show that such people existed. Authorities were strategically going to introduce excerpts of me discussing adoption on recordings, which they had seized from my car. I knew that one of those tapes contained a conversation between me and another individual named John Guillotte of Fairhaven, MA, which not only confirmed that others knew about my adoption, it also showed that my mind was actively suppressing information related to the subject in the spring of 1989.

I alerted my attorney to the corroborating conversation, which was contained on one of the tapes and insisted that it be introduced as evidence in support of my intended testimony. I next observed the prosecution listening to the tapes in the courtroom and was later informed by my attorney that no such conversation could be found on any of the recordings. It was a devastating blow but, no surprise that the prosecutors would deny the existence of evidence, which revealed the truth when they had worked so hard to conceal it. Whether it was just another lie or the evidence was actually destroyed didn't matter. It meant that my only proof was off the table and I assumed lost forever.

There was one other chance to corroborate the fact that some psycho had brainwashed me but it came with a catch. If all else failed, the individuals who came forward to my attorney when I was first arrested would testify to the truth but only in the aftermath of a conviction. This understanding was reiterated by my attorney who, after insisting that I let the trial proceed on its current course, assured me that any possible conviction would be immediately overturned by exposing the prosecution's false portrayal of the facts surrounding the case. Unfortunately, my treacherous attorney's compliance with that false narrative had painted me into a corner. With no way of forcing my reluctant backup witnesses to reveal the truth at trial, I had no choice but to let things play out on their terms and hope that they would come through for me as promised if the whole thing went south.

At one point in the trial, the deceptive tactics of the prosecution took a darker and more sinister turn when they displayed graphic photos in the courtroom, depicting postmortem thermal injuries to promote a false finding by their colleague in the Medical Examiner's Office that death resulted from thermal exposure in addition to smoke inhalation. In his report, the Medical Examiner found traces of soot in the airways and lethal levels of carbon monoxide in the bloodstream, which is consistent with death from smoke inhalation. However, he found no traces of thermal injuries to the airways, which is a key factor in establishing death due to thermal exposure. This shows that the victims of the deadly fire had already succumbed to smoke inhalation and were no longer breathing when their bodies were exposed to the superheated air that caused the horrific outer thermal injuries depicted in the photos. This evidence is supported by the first eyewitnesses on the scene who described the fire as being located on the south side of the house while all signs of life had already ceased from within. The occupants were later located in the north end of the home where the fire eventually reached after burning for an additional twenty minutes before being extinguished.

To the friends and family members of anyone who perishes in a house fire, there is little comfort in knowing that they died from smoke inhalation when considering the horror of being trapped in a burning building. However, it is beyond callous and cruel for a prosecutor to conjure up false images of someone burning alive in order to invoke an emotional response from jurors, with total disregard for the emotions of others.

In the end, conviction was a foregone conclusion and deliberations merely a formality, judging by the two hours and ten minutes that the jury spent deciding my fate before returning to the courtroom and pulling the lever. Although the head-snapping verdict was sudden and swift, there is no reason to think that further contemplation would have produced a different result considering the fact that no one can be expected to see the truth when they've been kept in the dark and told nothing but lies.

My Story—Jonathan B Taylor

While lies provided a foundation for the jury's misconception of the case against me, it was what they didn't hear that caused the most devastating damage. The jurors never heard the truth regarding my adoption and hypnosis from any of the countless witnesses with firsthand knowledge who could have exposed the fact that the prosecution's entire case was based on a lie. There was no mention of the man who had hypnotized me or the convenient vanishing act that he pulled around the time of the fire, leaving behind only the faintest traces of his existence such as an old canvas tarp and a tape recorded conversation that corroborated the fact that my mind had been previously suppressing information relating to my adoption. They never even heard about my resurfaced memories and were left with the impression that I just got it in my head one day that I was adopted and hypnotized without any explanation of what brought me to that conclusion. This was in part because the prosecutor was walking a line between presenting evidence to show that I believed I had been brainwashed without revealing it to be true while simultaneously convincing the jury that I was crazy enough to commit murder but not too crazy to be held accountable.

Of all the silence that stifled the truth, it was my own, which appeared the most deafening. Being duped into not testifying meant that the jury never heard any explanation for what I was doing in the

My Story—Jonathan B Taylor

woods for so long or how I ended up there in the first place. They never heard about my crossbow or stun gun because the judge suppressed those items for being prejudicial and having nothing to do with the alleged crime.

If I hadn't been sidelined, I would have brought truth and transparency to the stand, regardless of anyone's appetite for it. I would have related my experience of being overwhelmed with resurfacing memories, which revealed the hidden horrors of my past and then I would have called out those who had corroborated the recovered recollections whether they were ready to admit it or not. I also would have admitted to the hostility that I had toward those responsible for what was done to me, despite my attorney's attempts to downplay that animosity. Although it may have made me seem less empathetic, as it can sometimes be difficult to muster sorrow for those who have committed unspeakable acts of evil against you, it certainly didn't set me in motion to commit murder. Yes, I wanted them to be held accountable but if anything, I needed them alive and had no interest in seeing anyone lose their lives. In spite of our horrifying history, this was undoubtedly a terrible tragedy and, while my antagonists may have made some despicable choices, I still saw them as manipulated victims of the same evil master who preyed upon me.

My Story—Jonathan B Taylor

I can't say if my testimony would have changed any minds on the jury. Trying to convince them of the truth regarding my adoption and hypnosis without any proof could have just fed into the false narrative of the prosecutor and my attorney that I was deranged and delusional regarding those matters. Only the jurors themselves could say if they would have seen things differently had they known the actual truth.

Following my conviction, I looked to those individuals who had come forward to my attorney to make good on the assurance that they would reverse the conviction by revealing the truth. However, only a fool trusts in the hearts of cowards and it was soon evident that my reluctant liberators would remain in the shadows and leave me for dead. There was a brief glimmer of hope when I was visited by one of the backsliders named Francis (Frank) Mahady of Mattapoisett who vowed to rescue me from my wrongful conviction and see the prosecutor charged with perjury for his criminal misrepresentations. I later learned that that he would not be speaking up for fear of reprisals. One note of interest on this particular individual is how he once showed me a letter that he wrote to investigators of the New Bedford Highway Killings in, which he described the scene of my brother running from the woods to a gray van parked on the shoulder. Apparently, he too had been on the highway that day and witnessed the same thing that I had seen. This confirmed my own resurfaced memory of the incident and demonstrated a willingness on the part of authorities to overlook some perceivable connections to those crimes. However, it should be noted that, in spite of his reckless attempts to implicate himself, we know that individual could not possibly be the Highway Killer due to the fact that he was armed with the perfect alibi. He was in jail awaiting trial on a separate murder charge of, which he was later acquitted, during the time that victims of the Highway Killer were disappearing. You can be sure that this was not by coincidence but rather by design

I knew that I was in trouble when the individuals who were supposed to expose the truth and have my conviction instantly overturned, started talking about waiting to see what happened with the direct appeal, which was a process that could take years to play out. There was one outrageous suggestion that a belief in my innocence was the only thing stopping those unwilling witnesses from revealing the truth. As long as they were sure that the fire was an accident, they could continue to imagine that there was nothing wrong with brainwashing a child and avoid publicly having to acknowledge their own participation in the treachery. However, if it was believed that I actually had committed murder, then they would be compelled to put a stop to the disturbing mind game that could have culminated in such a crime. By this backward thinking, they would be willing to let me rot in prison for something that I didn't do while, only coming to my rescue for something that they thought I did.

My Story—Jonathan B Taylor

It seemed like an odd predicament but the dilemma of admitting to something you didn't do is actually faced by many wrongfully convicted individuals since those who are serving second-degree life sentences are generally expected to take responsibility for the crimes they are accused of committing as a prerequisite to obtaining parole. The concept of providing a confession in exchange for the truth being exposed about my adoption and hypnosis was first introduced by my attorney when he visited me in lockup following my initial arrest. At the time, I had no intention of admitting to something that I didn't do in order to trigger the truth to be revealed. However, a new set of circumstances had left me with nothing to lose and I was desperate enough to try anything that could stop the train from barreling off the cliff. I figured that I could give them their false confession and once the truth was out, I could recant. My journey down this road was short lived and I found myself unable to follow through with the plan. Even if there was a chance of making it all go away, I couldn't bring myself to claim responsibility for something I didn't do. It only had a slim chance of succeeding anyway with it's reliance on a group of individuals who had repeatedly shown an unwillingness to do the right thing. Besides, they were still putting everything on my birth mother and hiding behind the excuse that she should be the one to reveal the truth when in fact, it was the hypnotist and his helpers who had caused all the chaos. If their goal was to punish my birth mother

My Story—Jonathan B Taylor

for revealing the truth of my adoption to me when I was five then why did I seem to be the one suffering all of the consequences for her actions?

At one point, while I was awaiting trial, a plea bargain offer was made by the Prosecutor, Paul Dawley through my attorney at the time, Kevin Reddington who had been brought on for a motions hearing in, which my court appointed attorney, Joseph Krowski, Sr. was scheduled to appear as a witness. During a meeting in Attorney Reddington's office, he informed me that Mr. Dawley had made an offer of twelve to twenty years if I was willing to plead guilty to manslaughter, which under the old law would have meant serving around eleven years in prison for something I didn't do. Knowing what was at stake, I declined that offer and took a leap of faith for, which I paid the ultimate price. I sometimes wondered if the Prosecutor made that offer in an attempt to ease his own conscience for what was being done to me but that would assume that he ever had one in the fist place.

However, I was still haunted by the fact that my birth mother's actions before and after the fire showed that she wanted me to be in this hopeless situation where all signs were seemingly pointed to an absurd notion that claiming responsibility for something I didn't do would somehow provide a way out. If she had set all of this up, was I

My Story—Jonathan B Taylor

expected to take that final step that would initiate the truth coming out or was it just another trap meant to ensnare me further? And, what was her backup plan if I didn't take the bait? Was she going to leave me here to rot like everyone else was willing to do? She had also told me that one of her tasks would be to prevent me from acquiring proof of my adoption from anything she had done and having me locked up in prison certainly accomplished that.

In the years that followed the aftermath of my conviction, I've fought futilely for exoneration while those who could free me with a few simple words have gone about their lives in complete indifference. Their silence has robbed me of decades and allowed a corrupt prosecutor and defense attorney to go unchecked, creating unknown numbers of other wrongful convictions in their wake.

Although my fight for freedom has met a wall at every turn, I continue to battle the invisible dragon while blindfolded, shackled and armed with only a quill. Through my efforts, I learned of a mystery witness who reported seeing a black car racing from the Crescent Beach area around the time of the fire. This was significant because it corroborated my own account of hearing a car tearing out of the Channel Street area just before I discovered the fire. Two other witnesses were quoted on page 14 of Trooper Joe Mason's report as claiming to have heard 'what sounded like tires screeching' at that

My Story—Jonathan B Taylor

same time and were listed as defense witnesses but never called by my attorney to testify. I later learned that one of those witnesses was the one who saw the black car although there was no mention of it in the police report. There is no question that a car tearing out of a mostly deserted community at 4:30 in the morning would seem peculiar under any circumstances but the timing and location in this particular case are what make it more than just a little suspicious.

In other discoveries, I learned that the authorities had concocted a story in, which they claimed to have actually found two melted gas cans in the debris but were only allowed to present evidence of one. This claim was made by Richard Taylor Jr. and appears to be an underhanded attempt to turn supportive witnesses against me by trying to convince them that the fire was not an accident. This type of deceptive tactic is often used by investigators to turn suspects on one another and with no public admonishments over the practice, it continues to take a toll on the wrongfully accused. It could also be that this story was concocted to counteract the discrepancy in the Commonwealth's case concerning the fact that only one gas can was found at the scene. This would provide an imaginary explanation for why there was only one can being discussed at trial in case any of their witnesses, whom they needed to convince of my guilt in order to ensure their cooperation, questioned the inconsistency.

My Story—Jonathan B Taylor

In another twist, they changed the law in 2007, making it possible for Massachusetts adoptees to obtain copies of their original unamended birth certificates. Although this wouldn't prove that I was hypnotized, it would allow me to show that the prosecutor perjured himself regarding my adoption. In December of 2014, I applied for a copy of my original unamended birth certificate and five months later I received an undated response from a woman of unknown job title named Katherine (Kathy) Serrano on Registry of Vital Records and Statistics letterhead claiming that no amendment to my birth record could be found. I had already confirmed the fact that I was adopted so this was about acquiring proof, which apparently the Commonwealth wasn't prepared to provide.

One of the greatest hindrances on my struggle for freedom was imposed by my former attorney when he failed to turn over my trial file, which is an essential tool in any post conviction campaign. Although a request for assistance from the Bar Overseers failed to produce any of the missing documents, it did prompt my former attorney to relinquish four cassette tapes that were in his possession and turned out to contain copies of the original tapes that were seized from my car. Upon reviewing the long lost discovery materials in the prison law library, I discovered that one of the tapes contained the conversation corroborating my adoption and hypnosis, which the prosecutor and my attorney claimed could not be located on the

My Story—Jonathan B Taylor

originals. Somehow, it had survived and was in my attorney's possession the whole time. Despite the efforts to cover their tracks, they had let a crucial piece of evidence slip through their fingers and right into my hands.

It's one thing to have proof but it's another to be able to use it and in order to do that, you need to find someone who will listen. With no other options available, I turned to the Committee for Public Counsel Services, which was the same state agency that had given me my trial attorney and continued to unleash him on unsuspecting defendants in capital cases. It was no surprise when they rejected my October 2018 request for assistance. However, I was not expecting Elizabeth Dembitzer, the woman who made the call, to go a step further and assert that even if I could prove that the prosecutor lied about my adoption and hypnosis, it would not be grounds for reversal because the question before the jury was whether or not I had set the fire. The suggestion that my being brainwashed by a man who disappeared around the time of the fire had no bearing on the case was baffling to me and extremely frustrating because, it was that line of thinking that allowed the Prosecutor to get away with his fraudulent portrayal of the facts and it meant that CPCS was backing his deceitful play.

I was confused by the Staff Counsel's conclusion because the case law states that a conviction can be reversed over the presentation

My Story—Jonathan B Taylor

of any false or misleading evidence, which might have been a factor in the jury's deliberations. Only the jury can know if they would have been influenced by the knowledge that the prosecutor deceived them. Of course, nobody wants to think that they condemned an innocent person to die in prison so it's easier to convince themselves that they made the right call. However, if even one juror acknowledged that they might have thought differently had they known the truth about my being brainwashed and the abrupt absence of the man responsible, it could overturn my conviction and give me a shot at a fair trial where the truth might actually have a chance to prevail.

Throughout my life, I was under attack from lies, which culminated in a final barrage meant to annihilate me at trial. While the lies had done a number on me, it was silence that proved to be my greatest enemy. With silence stifling the truth, there was nothing to stop the lies from flourishing. Telling 'My Story' is about breaking that silence and revealing the truth no matter what the result. An attorney would say that in the world of perception, total transparency is a risky endeavor. However, there is little to risk when you have nothing left to lose.

For those who know the truth and have perpetuated the lie through either their words or their silence, I think of the decades that their contribution has cost me and wonder how they are able to exist

My Story—Jonathan B Taylor

without a soul. It's been said that it's one thing to know that you can't find anyone who is willing to do something despicable for you but if you can't find one person who is willing to do something righteous for you, then you truly are alone.

My Story—Jonathan B Taylor

Afterword

I set out on the path of revelation with a monumental task before me. I was attempting to expose the truth of what was done to me at the same time as I was trying to change the hearts and minds of the very people I was calling out for playing a role. While it may sound simple, finding the words to tell my story was excruciating and people aren't always receptive to the concepts of truth and honesty in a harsh universe where fear and skepticism fill the void.

Placing a message in a bottle and casting it into the sea without knowing if that message will ever reach anyone is an undeniable act of desperation. As my words float aimlessly across a chasm in hopes of being heard, somewhere out there lurks an army with the power to free me sheathed tightly at their sides. Despite astounding numbers and the truth clenched in their teeth and hands, these hollow heroes remain frozen like empty suits of armor with echoes in place of hearts. Cold blooded cowards who would lay down like desolate highways with yellow stripes down their backs, when they should stand.

Perched precariously upon a trapdoor, pending a plunge into darkness, I curse my captors and their quiet cohorts who dance before me in a sea of black holes with toothy grins and sinewy claws that

My Story—Jonathan B Taylor

scratch at the lever. Caped and cowled demons wielding spiked scythes who have declared war on my soul.

I no longer recognize friend from foe as the battle lines have blurred between my allies and adversaries who now stand united in silence. In my quest to bring the truth to light, I have descended down into the pit to reach the level of my enemies in vain attempts to draw them from beneath their rocks, only to see them smile at my suffering and take pleasure in watching me struggle against my binds as the tracks begin to rattle.

The time for providing amusement with pointless pleadings to gleeful tormentors has reached its end as the curtain closes on those wasted efforts and the remnants of my urgings finally fall silent. Whatever mysterious motivation wriggles through the minds of my enemies and drives them to inflict such sadistic evil upon me is beyond comprehension. They act as if fueled by hatred while hell bent on vengeance although it is unclear why I should be the recipient of that rage or what would possibly possess them to ever take it this far.

I've lost sight of everyone who had a hand in this as all lines to the past have been severed and even those who were once willing to reveal the truth and thought to be pulling for me have either gone dark or lie dormant. For now, it seems that their secret is safe and remains

My Story—Jonathan B Taylor

in the shadows, impervious to all attempts at exposure. However, the strange force that somehow stifles my story is sustained by my existence, subjecting it to a shelf life, which expires when I do and guarantees that when I'm gone, there will be nothing left to stop the truth from rising. Eventually, all will be revealed, including those details of my story that were too mind boggling to mention. The only question is whether I'll be around to see it?

At this point, it appears that my opponents have no intention of ever coming clean while I'm alive and many would probably prefer to have the truth be buried along with me as the only perceivable witness who could tie them to the crime. When the clock finally runs out on these culprits and the truth finds its way to the forefront, either through my doing or by way of my demise, there will be nowhere to hide for any conspirator whose undeniable involvement could place them in the crosshairs of public scrutiny where a minefield of questions awaits. Before they begin dancing in front of a firing squad, they should realize that it's always better to get out ahead of the truth than to let the truth get out ahead of you. Once the truth is knocking at your door, redemption is already out the window.

With no help on the horizon from anyone whose firsthand knowledge of my situation could free me, I look to those who have no familiarity with my story and are being brought into the fold for

My Story—Jonathan B Taylor

the first time through my induction. Unlike others who have been sworn to secrecy upon discovering the truth in the shadows, these innocent bystanders have no allegiance and are free to share what they have learned with whomever they choose. Absent any guilt or otherworldly parameters set forth by some self-professed master planner, they could provide a foothold for the truth to begin its final ascent toward total exposure.

While one head of the monster already knows the truth and only needs to be convinced of developing a conscience, the other is completely in the dark and has a more difficult road to enlightenment. Unfortunately, mine is an impossible tale that is fraught with too many unanswered questions and head scratching coincidences designed to disillusion even the most open-minded individual. I understand why anyone who stumbles across my story for the first time may be skeptical since I have often wondered myself how it is even possible that something like this could ever be allowed to happen. However, I don't have the luxury of doubt having lived through the experience and being forced to face the reality of it every day.

It's difficult to imagine how something this vast could have permeated and corrupted so many while somehow staying below the radar. Traveling by whisper and murmur like an old-time urban

My Story—Jonathan B Taylor

legend has kept my story off the grid and allowed it to remain in the shadows where there is no way of knowing just how far the darkness has spread or how many people it has enveloped. This open account shines a light on my story for the first time in a public arena where anyone can access its raw form without the conditions imposed by filters or constraints.

When the truth is hard to swallow, people often look for the easy solution to that which they don't understand and applying plausible explanations to an incomprehensible situation provides an imagined sense of order to an otherwise chaotic reality. Filling in the holes with uninformed suppositions about my sincerity or my rationality only serves to discredit me and move us further from the truth and deeper into the realm of doubt where unanswered questions and false narratives become truth and revelation's downfall.

I make no apologies for stating fact and don't answer to anyone who has capitalized on my compromised condition for things I may have said or done while under the influence of another. My story is real and everything happened just as I described it. Many of these people are still out there and know this to be true. For the unknowing, the tendency to dismiss my disturbing tale in favor of a more user friendly fallacy may seem like an alluring alternative to the truth but

My Story—Jonathan B Taylor

in order to defeat evil and corruption of this magnitude, we must first acknowledge that they exist.

To the skeptic, the idea of trying to change the world with only our words is like throwing darts at the moon but for the believer, words are like a rocket ship and provide the perfect pathway to launching a revolution.

My Story—Jonathan B Taylor

Appendix

As I related in the telling of 'My Story', there was a copy of a tape recorded conversation that I obtained from my former defense attorney, which had been seized by authorities from my car in 1993 and was thought to have been lost or destroyed. In this conversation, the individual with whom I'm speaking confirms my recollection of resurfaced memories involving references to me being adopted. Although this may not substantiate all of my assertions made in this book, it does provide corroboration that my mind was actively suppressing information related to the subject of adoption in the spring of 1989. This also shows that there was either a consorted effort by certain individuals to convince me that I was adopted when I really wasn't or, a wide spread effort to convince me that I wasn't adopted when I was. Although there is no conceivable reason to imagine why anyone would want me to believe that I was adopted if I wasn't, there is a dark and disturbing motive for why someone may want to convince me that I wasn't adopted when I actually was.

While there have been numerous individuals who have confirmed the validity of my resurfaced memories regarding adoption, I'm not sure what led me to secretly record this particular conversation or how it managed to survive all these years and ultimately find its way back into my possession. However, there is

My Story—Jonathan B Taylor

something undoubtedly ominous about its existence for, which I could not have foreseen the future significance of at the time of its creation.

In accordance with my intentions of full disclosure, I'm including a transcript of the relevant portions of that conversation in this text and in order to put this transcript in some form of context, I will begin by providing some background information to set the scene.

In the early spring of 1989, I was working for a couple of plasterers named John Guillotte of Fairhaven, MA and 'Buddy' Harding of Rochester, MA on a job site in the town of Plymouth, MA, not far from the Cape Cod Canal. During this time, Buddy made several remarks to me regarding my being adopted although my mind was actively suppressing information related to the subject of adoption at that time so I had no immediate recollection of his remarks in the moments after he made them. It wasn't until weeks later when I was no longer working for John and Buddy that I began to experience the resurfacing of hundreds of suppressed memories related to my adoption. It was during that period when I recalled Buddy's remarks and tracked him down to find out what he knew. Unfortunately, Buddy denied ever making those remarks but in a subsequent phone conversation with John G., he confirmed that Buddy did make those comments just as I remembered.

My Story—Jonathan B Taylor

A few months later, I tracked down John G. in person and secretly recorded our conversation as we discussed the events that occurred while working at the Plymouth job site and Buddy's remarks concerning the subject of me being adopted. Although he continued to confirm my resurfaced recollections of Buddy's remarks about my adoption, John was reluctant to acknowledge everything he knew and seemed intent on sticking to a script by repeatedly making the assertions that 'Buddy was only bullshitting' and assuring me that he 'would try to talk to him and find something out.'

Even if Buddy had been 'only bullshitting' about me being adopted, that didn't explain why he was saying those things or why my mind had suppressed the information just as it had done with every other incident related to the subject of adoption in the years leading up to those disclosures. Additionally, some of Buddy's statements were consistent with other facts surrounding my adoption. He knew that I had siblings who were adopted and there was an allusion made to me having a brother. He also identified my birth mother who by no coincidence was operating a street cleaner for an asphalt maintenance company in a parking lot near the job site.

There were other references made by Buddy, including some about my birth father who happened to be driving the truck that delivered building materials to the construction site. Although John was willing to confirm the sighting of my birth mother, he refused to corroborate any information concerning my birth father, even making a feeble attempt at being unable to pronounce his name before blurting it out with obvious familiarity moments later on the tape.

The fact that Buddy knew so many details about my adoption meant that he obviously knew about my being hypnotized as a child to conceal it from me, which is why he felt so comfortable lying to my face when it came to denying his remarks about me being adopted. I was also sure that John knew more than he was letting on as both he and Buddy would have witnessed my eyes flashing through their memory scrubbing sequence at the time that Buddy was making those provocative comments. It was unclear why John would acknowledge some things while denying others but I was grateful for the honesty that he did provide in spite of his otherwise evasiveness.

Because this conversation was being recorded on a device that was concealed in my coat pocket, there are gaps in some parts of the audio that could have resulted from me leaning or shifting in a way, which may have muffled the sound. Although I have some recollection of what was said during those inaudible portions, I only included the verifiable dialogue in the process of drafting this transcript. The following is a copy of that draft.

My Story—Jonathan B Taylor

Transcript of conversation between John Guillotte and Jonathan Taylor recorded sometime during the winter of 1990:

J.T.: But, I wanted to talk to you. You must know what I wanted to talk to you about.

J.G.: About you being adopted? I don't know anything about it.

J.T.: Just what he said. (Buddy)

J.G.: I've already talked to Buddy. He said, "That kid's fucked up." He's only bullshitting you. He's only bullshitting you.

J.T.: Yeah but he had that (inaudible) down there, and about Paul Pothier? Remember that guy, right? You said you did.

J.G.: Paul Pothier?

J.T.: Yeah.

J.G.: Oh, the kid you talked to me about? You told me about?

J.T.: No. He was the one that was deliverin' the blue boards.

J.G.: From Humphrey's? (building supply company)

J.T.: Yeah.

J.G.: Doesn't sound familiar.

J.T.: He's a plasterer. Owns a plastering business. 'Cause I remember we went over to check out the other one (condominium unit), and then we went back and you said you saw Paul Pothier over there.

J.G.: Oh, I might know who he is but the name don't sound familiar. But I talked to Buddy about that but said he was only shitting

My Story—Jonathan B Taylor

around, you know? Because you said, "Try to find out for me." So, I went I went up to him one morning. He was doing a job for me and it popped into my head. I said, "Buddy," I said, "I talked to Jonathan. What was all that shit you said about Jonathan being adopted?" He said, "I was just fuckin' with his head. He still believes it?" I go, "I don't know." Did he go talk to you? Did you talk to him?

J.T.: Yeah. He said you're lyin'.

J.G.: I'm not lyin'!

J.T.: I know that. I was right there too. He said he never said any of that. But, I just want to know who fuckin' told him that. You know? And, I remember him telling you, "Paul told me."

J.G.: Maybe…(inaudible)

J.T.: Could have been. I don't know.

J.G.: Are you adopted?

J.T.: That girl on the street cleaner. He said, "That's his mother."

J.G.: I forgot the whole story.

J.T.: No, you remember it, 'cause you remembered it this summer.

J.G.: Yeah, but I forget. I forget.

J.T.: Come on John, man.

J.G.: I'm serious. What street cleaner? Who's the street cleaner?

J.T.: Remember the girl on the street cleaner with the black hair. She was riding the street cleaner and you said, "Buddy, look at the girl on the street cleaner".

J.G.: Oh, yeah. Yeah.

J.T.: And he (Buddy) goes, "That's his mother."

J.G.: Oh, yeah.

J.T.: Well, that's the same girl who supposedly is my mother. Don't you think that's a coincidence or what?

J.G.: It probably is a coincidence.

J.T.: But, he was just goofing around saying that? Then it turns out to be true. You know what I mean?

J.G.: Well…

J.T.: But, then there was something else he told you. All right, since we're not taking any of this seriously, I want to know what else he said, 'cause…

J.G.: I have no idea.

J.T.: No. Come on.

J.G.: I'll talk to him. I'm doing a job for him.

J.T.: No. He won't tell you anything. He's an asshole.

J.G.: Yes he will. He will so.

J.T.: He sucks. I hate that fuckin' asshole.

J.G.: Me and Buddy, we just got done with a job.

J.T.: (interrupting) When, um, remember there was some kid backing a van up, right, and you came out and you said, "What, do you think that kid's your brother?" and you were laughin' at me? You don't remember that? And, I said, "No. Why?"

J.G.: Oh, yeah, yeah, yeah. Where were we? At McDonald's?

My Story—Jonathan B Taylor

J.T.: No. This was right at the job site. And you said, "No, I was just thinkin' of something that Buddy told me", and you were laughin'.

J.G.: Oh, yeah. Alright, yeah.

J.T.: What did he tell you though?

J.G.: That was about that. About you being... I don't know. You being adopted or something. I don't know.

J.T.: He didn't tell you the whole story though?

J.G.: He didn't tell me nothin'. All I know is the part that you told me. The bits and pieces that you told me. That's all I know.

J.T.: And what he (Buddy) said.

J.G.: And then I asked him, 'cause you called me and you talked about it so I asked him. He said he didn't know anything about you being adopted, he was just pulling your leg. And that's all he told me. But I'll look into it.

J.T.: You don't remember him saying that guy, Paul Pothier that was deliverin' blue boards?

J.G.: I don't remember him. I remember there was a street cleaning girl. I remember that. But I don't remember about that other stuff. Paul Poth, Poth, Pothier?

J.T: Can you remember him (Buddy) sayin', "Aren't some of you adopted?" to me? And I was like, then I hated him after he said it.

J.G.: Yeah.

My Story—Jonathan B Taylor

J.T.: Then, he got me in the van and he was like, "Jonathan has four sisters and he looks just like them." And then I smiled and everything was cool.

J.G.: Yeah. Yeah.

J.T.: Don't you think that was pretty weird behavior?

J.G.: Well, I don't…

J.T.: I think it was weird. (getting aggravated) All right John, man, I'm sorry to bother you. Forget it.

J.G.: I don't know the story, because I never talked anything to do with Buddy, all I ever did was just ask him. I said, "Do you know anything about Jonathan being adopted?" And he said, "I was just bullshitting with him." You know. And I never even brought up the street cleaning girl, or this Pothier. What's his first name? Paul?

J.T.: Paul Pothier

J.G.: Oh, tomorrow…

J.T.: (interrupting) You know a plastering company called Artistic Drywall and Stucco in Fairhaven on Water Street?

J.G.: No. That's not Paul Pothier. Artistic Plaster is Bragga. (inaudible) I just worked with him. About a month and a half back, I worked two weeks straight with Denis Bragga. It's called Artistic Plastering and Stucco.

J.T.: Really? And he prints an ad in the paper like yours?

J.G.: Yeah. And he lives right on Water Street.

My Story—Jonathan B Taylor

J.T.: Oh, that musta' been why he was aggravated. 'Cause I called there to ask for you because I got your number out of the paper. That was awhile ago though. He was like, "No! John isn't here!" He was like all pissed off.

J.G.: "Cause he knew. He knows who I am. No, but I'll find out 'cause I'm doin' a job with Buddy. I'm gonna talk to him about it. You know, he talks straight with me about everything. He talks to me different than he talks to everybody else. He lets me in on shit that he wouldn't let anybody else in on. You know, like as far as women and shit. He talks to me about old girlfriends and he'll even say to me, "Don't say nothin' to anybody else about it." You know. I talk straight out to him, so I'll find out.

J.T.: But, this is fucked up man, 'cause other people said it too man.

J.G.: I wouldn't even worry about it. Do you look like your sisters?

J.T.: A little, but not like I look like that girl on the street cleaner. (you saw)

J.G.: Yeah, but that don't matter. Shit, I've seen people that look more like my brother…

J.T.: (interrupting) No, no, no. I told you about when I was fifteen and I was at City Hall and the guy said, "One of you was adopted."

J.G.: (interrupting) And you saw the girl. That woman was there. Looked like the street cleaner?

My Story—Jonathan B Taylor

J.T.: Well, that happened afterwards. That happened later. But, before that, I was at City Hall right, and the guy with the birth records...

J.G.: (interrupting) Are you sure you weren't dreamin'? Were you high or somethin'?

J.T.: What do you mean, dreaming?

J.G.: Were you havin' a nightmare or somethin'?

J.T.: Yeah, fuckin' it is a nightmare.

J.G.: I wouldn't even worry about it. Why should you worry? Why should you...

J.T.: I tried to forget about it but that girl was driving the street cleaner fuckin' drives by the gas station all day long man.

J.G.: Why don't you talk to her?

J.T.: She pulls in and I talk to her. Listen, when I first started coming out of it this summer and I was like, I went to her and I asked her, "Did you have a kid when you were fourteen?" And she was like, "I can't tell that Jonathan. Ask your mother. What did she say? Well Jesus Christ, you're fuckin' nineteen years old. You're old enough to know." So, I said, "Then it's true?" And she was like, "I can't tell you that." Now she says that I have her believing that shit.

J.G.: You know what you do. Get yourself... either act like a private detective, or hire somebody.

J.T.: I already got... I'm on probation...

My Story—Jonathan B Taylor

J.G.: I'll find out because... you know, it doesn't concern me, but... it's got me thinkin'. I'll look into it.

J.T.: I can't get on with my life. You know?

J.G.: You should get on with your life. I wouldn't worry about it too much. I mean, if I was going through life and didn't know I was adopted, and I'm twenty two now and I had these parents for all these years... I mean, why should I even try to find my fuckin' parents? 'Cause, if they were decent enough parents, they would come and tell me, hey, I'm your real mother or I'm you're real father.

J.T.: What if they can't? You know?

J.G.: That stuff's on soap operas. It's kind of silly. But, I'll find out.

J.T.: All right, John, man. Thanks. You've been a true friend.

My Story—Jonathan B Taylor

Important: Please Read

*Further Points of Emphasis:

The gas can and the gas station attendant:

One of the most disturbing and problematic pieces of evidence against me involves allegations made by a gas station attendant named Glenn LeBlanc, the State's star witness, who claimed that I walked into a local service station the day before the fire and attempted to purchase gasoline in a plastic milk jug.

As I previously stated, this is something I would never do. Having worked at a gas station myself, I'm fully aware that you can not put gas in a plastic milk jug. Nor would I ever have allowed someone else to do this if they were to come into the station where I once worked and make a similar attempt.

Although I've addressed some of the flaws with those false accusations, this is a closer look at the inconsistencies that show how Glenn was manipulating facts and manufacturing a storyline in an effort to make his false claims fit the evidence.

Here is the evidence as it was presented at trial:

My Story—Jonathan B Taylor

On May 13, 1993, the day before the fire, an individual who is described as 'a young man in his twenties with short dark hair', reportedly entered the Mattapoisett Mobil Station carrying a red plastic gas can along with a plastic milk jug and requested to purchase gasoline. Glenn LeBlanc, the attendant who was working the counter, told the man that he could fill the gas can but he could not put gas in the milk jug. When the man asked why he couldn't purchase gas in the milk jug, Glenn explained that it was illegal. Glenn then sent the man out to the pump and watched him to make sure that he didn't try to fill the milk jug. During this time, Glenn claims that the man was so inept that he was unable to operate the gas pump because he didn't know enough to pull back the vapor recovery sleeve and needed to be shown how to do this by another employee named David Hodges. At some point, Glenn also elaborated that he witnessed this person overfill the gas can in an effort to make the purchase an even $3.00. Then the man presumably put the gas can in his vehicle and left.

Five days later, on May 18, Detective Pina of the Mattapoisett Police Department visited the Mattapoisett Mobil Station and spoke to Glenn LeBlanc during, which time he asked him if anyone had come into the station on May 13 to purchase gasoline in a red plastic container. Glenn immediately recounted the incident involving the individual with the milk jug. Detective Pina then showed him a stack

My Story—Jonathan B Taylor

of photos from, which he identified my picture as the person he sold gas to that day. Two other witnesses, David Hodges and Reuben Woods remembered seeing the man with the milk jug and gave physical descriptions that were similar to me but neither identified me as that individual. However, David Hodges described the man's car as being similar to mine (small, beige) although his was 'old and rusty'. (Trial transcript pg. 4-302) It should be noted that when David Hodges was being asked by the Prosecutor to describe the vehicle at trial, he was never shown a picture of my car for positive identification purposes despite the fact that such pictures were entered into evidence through other witnesses in relation to it being towed and searched. (Trial transcript pg. 4-28) This was not an oversight by the prosecutor but obviously an intentional act to hide the fact that my vehicle didn't actually match the one that this other individual was driving.

Three days after that, on May 21, Troopers Joe Mason and Sgt. Kelleher of the State Police visited the Mattapoisett Mobil Station and spoke to Glenn LeBlanc. During this time, they asked him to review the cash register tape from May 13, 1993 and identify the record of the sale involving the individual with the milk jug. As I previously explained, authorities found the remnants of a 2.5 gallon red plastic gas container in the debris at the scene in the area of the front porch where a neighbor reported seeing it stored the previous day. Glenn

My Story—Jonathan B Taylor

looked through the tape and circled a $4.00 purchase for 3 gallons of gasoline. However, this is a problem because 3 gallons doesn't fit into a 2.5 gallon container. Glenn then circles a second purchase on the tape for 2.68 gallons of gasoline because he miraculously remembers that the individual purchased 'regular' instead of 'special'. The problem is that 2.68 gallons still doesn't fit into a 2.5 gallon container so, Glenn provides some more intricate details to account for the discrepancy by claiming that the individual kept pumping the gas in an effort to round the purchase off to an even $3.00, which led to the can being overfilled, causing some of the gasoline to spill out onto the ground.

There are several problems with Glenn's convenient scenario in, which he attempts to explain how a purchase of 2.68 gallons of gasoline could be made by someone with a 2.5 gallon can. First, is the fact that his explanation calls for .18 gallons or 23.27 oz., which is nearly 1/5 of a gallon to be intentionally spilled onto the ground. This would be like pouring a 24 oz. bottle of water out onto the ground, which would leave a substantial puddle but, when asked if he was concerned about this large puddle being left on the ground at trial, Glenn responded that 'It wasn't that much'. (Trial transcript pg. 4-271) Second, Glenn's attempt to clean up one inconsistency only leads to another. If the individual spilled gasoline all over the outside of this container and then presumably placed it in his vehicle, there would be traces of accelerants on the interior but, the state police canine went through the entire interior of my vehicle and found no traces of accelerant. (Trial transcript pg. 4-74)

Finally, and most importantly, Glenn's explanation isn't even possible for one simple fact. Even if someone was so determined to round off a number to an even $3.00 that they would intentionally continue pumping nearly a quart of gasoline into an overflowing container, there is a safety feature on the nozzle that prevents this scenario from taking place. All gas pump nozzles are fitted with sensors that automatically shut off the pump when the outside comes into contact with gasoline, which prevents overfilling. Unfortunately, this point wasn't challenged at trial and his factually infeasible testimony was allowed to stand.

Based on corroborating accounts, it is clear that someone who was at least somewhat similar in appearance to me walked into the Mattapoisett Mobil Station the week of the fire and attempted to purchase gasoline in a plastic milk jug. Although Glenn LeBlanc insists it was me, the fact remains that it was not. Despite the weight that eyewitness testimony is given in criminal prosecutions, it has been proven to be one of the most unreliable forms of evidence so, it would be easy to accept this as a case of mistaken identity. However,

My Story—Jonathan B Taylor

Glenn made several other assertions that don't add up and suggest something far more sinister.

Despite the fact that we both grew up in a small town and had come into contact with one another countless times over the course of our lifetimes, Glenn insisted that he didn't know who I was and 'didn't recall' ever seeing me before although he admits that it is possible he may have. This is the same individual who claimed to remember whether some random customer ordered 'regular' or 'special' gasoline more than a week after the purchase took place. Although Glenn and I were not friends, I was friends with his brother Craig when we were growing up and had an obvious familiarity with Glenn. I was also a frequent customer at Nick's Pizza where Glenn previously worked and had regular interactions with him during that time. For him to claim that he didn't recall ever seeing me before was clearly a lie. It's true that he would not have recognized me as a regular customer of the Mattapoisett Mobil Station because I never purchased my gas there due to the fact that their prices were too high so, why would I suddenly choose this day to make an exception?

Glenn also insisted that he didn't see any news reports of the fire in the days before he picked my photo out of the lineup, which seems highly unlikely considering the fact that this was a sizable event in a small town that wasn't accustomed to the extensive coverage that

My Story—Jonathan B Taylor

occurred in the local and regional newspaper and television outlets. He also claimed that he didn't know the significance of why he was being asked about the purchase of gasoline by Detective Pina or what it pertained to when he identified my photo, (12/22/94 motions hearing transcript pg. 78) despite admitting under cross-examination that he was aware of the fire and knew that I had been arrested the day before. (12/22/94 motions hearing transcript pgs. 93-94)

I don't know why Glenn would insist it was me who tried to purchase gas in a plastic milk jug that day but his other deceptions indicate a malicious willingness to pass off information that he knew to be false. For reasons that can only be known to him, it appears that when Detective Pina walked into the Mobil Station four days after the fire and asked if anyone had come in to purchase gasoline in a red plastic container the previous week, Glenn saw this as an opportunity and despite his insistence that he had no idea what the significance was in identifying my photo, common sense would say that he had to have known his accusations would place him right in the middle of this substantial event that was unfolding in our small town. These implausible denials could be a clumsy attempt at covering up his underlying motives.

Unfortunately, people will tend to dismiss Glenn's inconsistencies and overlook his lack of credibility while focusing entirely on the fact that he insisted I was the person he sold gas to on the day before the fire and basic human decency dictates that no one would ever make such a serious accusation if they weren't absolutely sure it was true. However, those individuals would be basing their conclusions on their own morality when in fact, basic standards of human decency don't fully apply to admitted pedophiles whose very nature is rooted in lies and manipulation.

To ingratiate himself in the community and place himself in a position of trust, Glenn created a false persona of the upstanding citizen by volunteering as a youth soccer coach and member of the Big Brother/Big Sister Program. His status was elevated even further by his perceived cooperation in the fraudulent criminal case that was being brought against me. Eventually, Glenn's deceitful nature became known about a year after I was convicted when he was arrested and charged with molesting three young boys, ages nine to eleven, who he gained access to through his volunteer work with various youth organizations. It was suspected that there may have been more victims but Glenn's quick admission and subsequent guilty plea to a three to six year sentence may have suppressed the need for further investigation and reduced the risk of additional victims coming forward.

My Story—Jonathan B Taylor

The idea that someone fitting my description would walk into a local service station and make a skeptical of himself in a botched attempt to purchase gas with a plastic milk jug the day before I'm accused of setting a fatal fire in that same small town is unsettling to say the least. However, if this was an intentional act to incriminate me, there were no guarantees that Glenn would mishandle the situation the way that he did.

I realize that these arguments may only serve to establish the fact that I wouldn't be foolish enough to try and purchase gas in a plastic milk jug or be incapable of operating a gas pump without assistance and in response, authorities could still make the case that it would have been possible for me to use the can of gas that was reportedly being stored on the front porch to start the fire in the way that they described. However, when facts are false and theories mistakenly surmised, you can often find holes in those scenarios, which will allow the truth to be exposed.

Traces of Accelerant:

From evidence that is not in dispute, we know that a melted 2.5 gallon red plastic container was found in the debris and that several areas tested positive for the presence of gasoline including areas of the foyer and stairway leading to the second floor. Investigators hypothesize that this would indicate that someone poured gasoline down the stairs and in the area of the foyer before somehow igniting it although they were unable to explain how the individual could have done this without being severely injured by the resulting fireball that would be sure to follow. Under cross-examination, the State's Arson Investigator, Sgt. Galizio suggested that someone could have tied a book of matches to a rock and thrown it from fifty feet away although he admitted that no such item was found. (Trial transcript pg. 2-307) In fact, the only type of potential ignition device that was ever identified during the trial was a mass of faulty wiring described as a 'spaghetti bowl', that wasn't up to code and showed multiple signs of arcing. This mass was located at the base of the stairwell, which is where Galizio determined the fire to have originated. During a sidebar, Judge Steadman refused to allow the State's electrical expert to rule this out as a possible cause during his testimony because he wasn't satisfied in his ability to do so. (Trial transcript pgs. 3-226 thru 3-231) It should also be noted that if someone had intentionally started the fire in the stairwell as Galizio suggests, then this would have placed them right in the middle of an area where gasoline was alleged to have been poured out over the floor. In these imagined scenarios, electrical malfunction would have to be the more likely method of ignition.

My Story—Jonathan B Taylor

While, the Commonwealth's theory is plausible, the evidence suggests otherwise. We know that an eyewitness reported seeing a gas can similar to the one that was found in the debris being stored in that same area on the day before the fire occurred. Another witness substantiated that gas was being stored on the front porch, which was serving as a base of operations in accordance with a brush clearing project that was taking place on the property. It is unclear how much gas was in this container but the fact that it was actively being used to fuel implements in a project would make it seem unlikely that the container was full at the time of the fire.

Knowing that gasoline was being stored in this location makes it reasonable to expect that traces of it would be found in the area following the fire. What's notable is the relatively small amount that was identified by investigators. If someone had poured 2.5 gallons of gasoline down the stairs and across the floor as authorities claim, then the entire area would have been saturated, leading to constant hits by the canine instead of the few random spots where alerts were actually made. It should also be noted that authorities continually referred to the melted gas can as being found 'inside of main front door' but under cross examination, Galizio admitted that the front door was completely gone and the container was located in the area where it was assumed to be based on the pile of debris. (Trial transcript pg. 2-292) However, the can was found melted into a small rug that was

My Story—Jonathan B Taylor

located outside the door on the front porch and served as a welcome mat for people to wipe their feet on before entering the home. (Trial transcript pgs. 6-133 thru 6-137)

Although the presence of the gas can on the front porch, would explain why traces of gasoline were found in that general area, it doesn't explain how they ended up in the three locations on the stairway. However, Gary Gaspar, the first firefighter to enter the house after the fire was extinguished, reported walking through that area before proceeding up the stairs, which could have potentially tracked the evidence along his path. (Trial transcript pgs 1-174 thru 1-175) Additionally, there were multiple personnel throughout the house before the stairway was secured by Galizio. It should also be noted that one of the samples was located on the second floor at the top of the stairs just a couple of feet away from the bed. Because, the second floor of the house was an open floor plan with only a banister and rails to divide the top flight of stairs from the living area, it means that in order to pour gasoline down those stairs as authorities suggest, someone would have to walk up and down a creaky flight of old wooden stairs in the dark, just feet away from where two people were known to be sleeping. It is also possible that gasoline could have been spilled and tracked through the house during the process of filling equipment on the front porch during the week.

My Story—Jonathan B Taylor

At trial, my defense attorney argued that the fire was accidental in nature and likely caused by a discarded cigarette on the front porch. However, the evidence suggests that the fire was more likely caused by faulty wiring located in the wall that sat between the base of the stairwell and the outside front porch where the gas can was being stored. This entire area was destroyed by fire and pummeled by fire hoses, which created a debris field leaving much of the evidence in disarray. In fact, the judge refused to allow the State's electrical expert to rule out electricity as a possible cause in his testimony based on his own observations of the evidence and his experience in trying arson cases. During a sidebar, Judge Steadman stated, "The problem with this case is it's such a destructive fire that it seems to have destroyed some of the evidence as to its cause". (Trial transcript pg. 3-237)

In addition to the traces of accelerant that were found at the scene, authorities also reported finding traces on my sneakers, which is not surprising considering the fact that I was a truck driver who pumped my own gas and fuel. Again, what is more significant is the lack of what was found. Taking into account that a canine's sense of smell is so sensitive that they have been known to track a human scent trail days after it was left, you would expect them to detect the remnants of some petroleum based products on my sneakers at any given time. Following his work at the scene, authorities had their canine go through my car and over all my clothing, which resulted in the sole

My Story—Jonathan B Taylor

alerts on my footwear. (Trial transcript pgs. 4-74 & 4-76) According to their accounts, the dog made precise indications on the upper laces area of one sneaker and the upper rear heal of the other by touching his nose to those particular locations. Curiously, the sneakers were never turned over so the canine was unable to indicate whether or not there were traces of petroleum on the bottoms. (Trial transcript pgs. 4-75 thru 4-76)

Authorities then made this a cornerstone of their case by suggesting that the presence of accelerant on the bottoms of the sneakers could have easily been picked up while fueling a vehicle at any self-service station but the presence of accelerant on the tops of the sneakers would indicate that it most likely got there by pouring gasoline from a can down a stairway and across a floor. However, as anyone who has ever pumped their own gas will know, when fueling a vehicle, there will always be drops left in the nozzle, which can easily drip onto a person's footwear or clothing when transferring it back to the pump. Therefore, if any traces were actually present on the tops of my sneakers as they suggest, I know that this is the only explanation for how they would have gotten there.

Unfortunately, the authorities' actions that followed during their testing procedure, call into question whether the canine ever actually made those precise indications and simultaneously prevent us from ever being able to prove otherwise. After the canine made its alleged alerts, all of the items were then brought to the State Crime Lab for corroborative chemical testing. During this procedure, items are placed in a device where they are heated to a specific temperature of approximately 180 degrees F for about twenty minutes so that any vapors that are produced can be extracted through electronic sensors that will detect trace amounts of accelerant as small as a human hair follicle. Because this is a process of extraction, the trace evidence is essentially removed from the item, thereby destroying it and making additional testing no longer an option.

Despite their intention to put all of the emphasis on the suggestion that the canine alerts were on the tops of the sneakers, investigators made no attempt to isolate those areas in the testing procedure. Instead of removing the laces and cutting swatches to test separately, they placed the entire sneaker in the machine making it impossible to ever confirm or counter those specific claims.

Knowing the willingness and ease with, which the authorities have misrepresented facts in this case, I don't believe this was just a simple case of carelessness on their part but rather a willful attempt to cover up another one of their underhanded moves. If they truly believed that there were traces of accelerant on the tops of those sneakers as they claim then you can be sure that they would have made it a priority to prove that assertion with a simple, standard step in the testing procedure rather than intentionally preventing the possibility of anyone ever being able to do so.

With their claims of specific canine alerts discredited by their subsequent actions, the only thing that the State's testing procedure proves is that microscopic traces of a petroleum based product were present on some unspecific portion of my sneakers. However, there were no other traces of accelerant found on any of my other clothing or inside of my vehicle. Therefore, rather than incriminate me, I believe that this evidence serves to exonerate me. If I had taken an overfilled gasoline soaked container and placed it in my vehicle during the day and then poured it down a flight of stairs and across a floor that night as authorities suggest, then there would have to be some evidence of this other than the microscopic traces that were identified on my footwear. I don't see how it would even be possible to handle a gasoline soaked container without getting any of it on your clothing or inside your vehicle. Nor does it seem likely that you could effectively pour it down a stairway or across a floor without the slightest bit splashing onto any part of your clothing besides your footwear. At the very least, you would expect there to be traces on the bottom portions of your pant legs.

My Story—Jonathan B Taylor

Unfortunately, I know that whatever arguments I make in support of my innocence will inevitably be challenged by those who wish to portray me as guilty while they continue to search for ever reaching alternatives to support their false accusations. Exposing the holes in one supposition will only lead to an alternative explanation with further contradictions in a vast sea of conjecture and endless hypotheticals.

For instance, one could make the case that it would be possible for someone to line the inside of their vehicle with plastic and somehow handle a gasoline soaked container in a manner, which prevented getting any of it on their hands or clothing. However, if one were being so careful, it is unlikely that they would have simultaneously made such a spectacle of themselves with a botched attempt to purchase gas in a plastic milk jug.

You could also argue that someone could very carefully pour 2.5 gallons of gasoline down a flight of stairs and across a floor as to avoid getting any on their clothing or simply change into another set of clothes. Again, I would point out that if someone were being so careful, it is unlikely that they would then leave a crossbow lying in the backyard or an errant arrow in the neighboring yard. Also, if someone were to go to the trouble of changing their clothes to conceal a crime, they would most likely change their footwear as well.

My Story—Jonathan B Taylor

Then, there is the issue of the single gas can that was found at the scene in the debris. We know that a neighbor reported seeing such a can in that same location the day before the fire so the question is; where is this other can that I'm accused of overfilling at the local Mobil Station while the known can was reported to be sitting on the front porch? I suppose that my accusers would argue that if the can on the porch was empty and needed to be filled then there might have been a window where I could have removed it from the porch and taken it to the local Mobil Station to fill without the neighbor or anyone else noticing it missing. However, this is another scenario that would make absolutely no sense. If I needed gas and wanted to fill a container for illicit purposes, then I certainly wouldn't take the risk of driving all the way to the local gas station in order to do this when I had gasoline available to me right there in the tank of my car, which I could have easily obtained in a matter of minutes by accessing the fuel line or simply siphoning it from the tank with a hose.

I realize that attacking my own arguments like this may not seem like the best move in the midst of a wrongful conviction claim but years of searching for answers has put me in this analytical mind frame where the moment I think of a point in my favor, I immediately find myself imagining a subsequent rebuttal. This may not help my case but acknowledging these things openly and confronting them head on is always the best policy and an important step in finding our way to the truth. Too often, when the evidence doesn't fit, people will look for ways to make it fit when what they should be doing is looking for the truth.

Unfortunately, one of the biggest challenges faced by the wrongfully convicted is the difficulty in trying to prove our actual innocence so, the most we can often hope to do is disprove the erroneous or misleading evidence against us.

The State's experts and their questionable conclusions:

The State's Arson Investigator, Gerard Galizio, testified that he determined the fire was an act of arson fueled by an accelerant, which originated in the stairway leading to the second floor. He based his conclusions on the amount of destruction to that area and an uneven burning of the stairs, which he claimed was indicative of a 'pour pattern' that was consistent with someone pouring gasoline down the stairs. However, under cross-examination he admitted that he never made any reference to a 'pour pattern' in either his report or in his testimony before the grand jury. (Trial transcript pgs. 2-287 thru 2-291) He also pointed to several areas in the stairway that showed signs of 'alligator charring', which he said was another indication of an accelerant being used although, under cross examination he acknowledged that alligator charring can be a result of intense heat and not necessarily the result of a flammable product. (Trial transcript pg. 2-272) He also conceded that there was alligator charring visible throughout the house and not just in the areas on the stairway. (Trial transcript pgs. 2-283 & 2-305)

In spite of Mr. Galizio's conclusions, there are many reasons in a fast moving fire why some portions of a stairway could sustain more damage than others. The fact that these were the original wooden stairs in an eighty-year-old house means that they were subject to a lot of wear and tear, which could cause some sections to burn more easily than others. One of the reasons that the fire spread so rapidly is because of the seasoned, old wood. Additionally, the currents of air being drawn in from the first floor and venting out into the second floor would feed the flames and concentrate the fire along their path in what is known as the 'chimney effect'. Although Mr. Galizio would like to portray his findings as an objective assessment of the scene based on scientific evidence, it is more likely that his conclusions were based on the presence of a melted gas can in the debris and his discussions with State Police detectives who had already towed my car before his investigation even began. From that point on, it was his job to come up with a scenario that supported their assumptions and created a case for arson.

My Story—Jonathan B Taylor

The same is true for James Rogers, the State's Electrical Investigator who claimed to have ruled out electricity as a contributing factor to the fire despite findings in his own report that contradict those assertions. At trial, the Judge prevented him from making that sweeping declaration because he wasn't satisfied in his ability to do so in relation to certain areas of the stairway where the fire is believed to have originated. Meanwhile, in his report, Mr. Rogers did admit to finding many violations of the electrical code and many fire hazards present but said that they did not 'appear' to contribute to the fire. He also said that many of the conducting connectors were improperly grounded and that some of the conductors in the area of origin showed signs of arcing but he didn't think they contributed to the fire because the outlet boxes showed no signs of internal heating. While those findings may serve to show that the fire was not caused by an overheating outlet box, they certainly don't eliminate the possibility that electricity may have contributed to the fire. Outlet boxes are not airtight devices and the fact that there was arcing in itself could be enough to ignite a fire. Especially in an area where gasoline was being stored and those fumes or vapors could have accumulated within the walls of a drafty old house. It also doesn't take an expert to know that any arcing, which occurs within a metal outlet box or an armor (metal) coated cable creates the potential for electricity to travel outside of that structure and possibly spark a fire. Additionally, Mr. Rogers noted that all but two of the circuit breakers had tripped to the 'off' position and determined that the conductors in the area of origin did not 'appear' to overheat from any internal electrical malfunctions and when they did overheat or develop short circuits the over current devices tripped. However, under cross examination Mr. Rogers admitted that he didn't follow any of the leads from the circuit breaker to the load they were servicing and therefore, couldn't confirm, which particular areas of the house had caused the breakers to trip or remain open. (Trial transcript pgs. 3-273 thru 3-274) He also conceded that he had no way of knowing when the arcing occurred or the circuit breakers were tripped so he couldn't say if it was before or after the fire had started. (Trial transcript pgs. 3-292 thru 3-293)

This still leaves the question of how gasoline ended up on the stairs. We know that three spots tested positive for the presence of gasoline on the stairs but those were in the same path that Gary Gaspar, the first firefighter to enter the scene described taking to reach the second floor after walking through an area where you could find contaminated suppression water, knowing that a can of gas was being stored in the area before the fire began. Considering the fact that the testing procedure used to detect the accelerant removes those traces by heating the sample to a mere 180 degrees Fahrenheit, it seems unlikely that the samples they took from the stairway, which were exposed to much higher temperatures during the fire would still have traces of accelerant present on them. However, if those traces were from the remnants of a melted plastic gas can that had been spread out over an area by suppression water from a fire hose before being tracked up the stairs by a firefighter after the fire had been extinguished then it would be reasonable to discover their presence in the results of such a testing procedure. Under cross-examination, the State's Chemist, John Drugan even admitted that it was an unusually high amount of trace elements to be found in items that had been exposed to such severe heat conditions. (Trial transcript pgs. 3-192 thru 3-194)

Deceitful Detectives and Their Treacherous Tactics:

One of the biggest contributors to wrongful conviction comes from a willingness on the part of authorities to bend the truth and manipulate facts in order to obtain a conviction at any cost. Like many of these cases, mine began with a rush to judgment by investigators who instantly viewed me as a suspect without actually knowing if a crime had even been committed. Once they convinced themselves of my guilt, they apparently felt justified in their efforts to falsify reports and commit acts of perjury in what may have been seen as a necessary evil in the overall quest for justice. In order to expose such acts of treachery, we look for traces of the truth to be hidden among the deceptions.

My Story—Jonathan B Taylor

For instance, when Trooper Joseph Mason, the lead investigator testified that I was not considered a suspect when they began searching for me in the woods, that is clearly a lie. (Trial transcript pg. 4-92) If I wasn't considered a suspect then why did he have my car towed at around 9:00 am, well before the search began? By his own admission, Trooper Mason claimed that he had my car towed because he saw a notebook with some writings inside, which he thought were possible evidence of a crime. (Affidavit for search warrant) Why would my writings be evidence of a crime if I was not considered a suspect and why were no other cars towed from the scene? His claims were further contradicted by the types of questions they were asking at our initial encounter. Trooper Scott Berna states that he asked me point blank if I hurt anyone back at the house. Why would he ask that if he didn't already suspect me of something?

Detectives lied about me not being a suspect in order to get around the fact that I was not issued a Miranda warning before they began peppering me with questions about the fire, which should have made any alleged statements inadmissible at trial. However, the Judge accepted the Detectives' claims that I was not considered a suspect and allowed the statements to stand although he found them to be ambiguous in nature. He also determined that I was not in custody at the time of the interrogation despite the Detectives' admission that I was not free to leave. (4/27/95 motions hearing transcript pg. 34) Some may view these obvious lies about me not being a suspect as harmless fabrications to get around nuisance Miranda requirements that handcuff authorities unnecessarily but the Court's indifference to such acts of perjury sends a dangerous message to investigators that if they can get away with one blatant lie then there is nothing to stop them from committing another.

Unfortunately, my attorney didn't properly dispute the statements in his efforts to have them excluded, which somehow gave the impression that I had confirmed them to be true when that was never actually the case. Although some of the Detectives' version of our encounter was accurate, many portions were omitted, twisted or completely fabricated. For example, when detectives claim they found me standing in a clearing with my hands in my pockets, that is not true. I was walking on the path when I encountered them and immediately put my hands in the air when they told me to 'Stop!' and appeared ready to draw their weapons.

Detectives also reported that I said 'You already know what happened' and I was preferably waiting to see a police officer when they confronted me. While I did say, 'You already know what happened', it wasn't in the context that they implied and, I certainly wasn't 'preferably' hoping to see a police officer although I knew that

My Story—Jonathan B Taylor

I was 'probably' going to encounter one. Where some of their accounts were only slight variations of the truth, others involved far more fabrication such as the claim that I said 'It's no fun hiding' when asked why I didn't run. This was actually a comment made by one of the officers that I admittedly may have agreed with due to my experience of being in the woods for that period of time.

The problem is, that these officers weren't taking any notes or recordings during our encounter and then claim to have sat down together later that day and crafted a transcript of our conversation based on their collective memories although the only record of that appears in Trooper Berna's report dated May 18, four days after we spoke. Rather than sitting down separately to ensure a fair and honest process, these two collaborated on their statement, which allowed them to avoid any inconsistencies while corroborating their different deviations from the truth. (Trial transcript pgs. 5-136 thru 5-137)

This makes it more difficult to prove those acts of deception when you have two detectives corroborating one another's claims but you can find evidence of their deceit in the presentation of their reports. For example, in the application for a search warrant on May 14, officers reported that I said 'You already know what happened' and I was 'preferably' waiting to speak with a police officer when they confronted me in the woods. There was never any claim that I said

My Story—Jonathan B Taylor

'It's no fun hiding'. That phrase doesn't appear anywhere until Scott Berna's May 18 report. If I had actually made that remark, you can be sure it would have taken precedence over the other two far less ominous quotes and been a highlight of their affidavit in support of the search warrant. The fact that it only appears as an afterthought in a subsequent report should demonstrate its lack of authenticity.

In the absence of any incriminating statements, detectives had to get creative in order to implicate me in the alleged crime. Although they did acknowledge that I told them I wasn't comfortable answering any questions in the woods, detectives continued to probe me in between random bits of small talk and then tried to imply that my silence was somehow a sign of guilt. They suggested that I gave 'no response' to certain questions, which is slightly misleading as I do remember nodding in the negative several times as opposed to providing no response at all. I'm not sure why I was reluctant to speak to them in that particular setting but something told me it was not a good idea and seeing how they twisted the truth and manipulated the facts in the aftermath of our encounter, it appears that I made the right call. I suppose I should consider myself fortunate that they stopped short of claiming I confessed because I would have no way of proving otherwise if they did.

My Story—Jonathan B Taylor

Further evidence of the Detectives' willingness to falsify facts can be seen in Trooper Joe Mason's May 27 report regarding the circumstances surrounding Glenn LeBlanc's May 21 identification of a May 13 gasoline purchase on a cash register tape. As I previously noted, there was a discrepancy in Glenn's identification of that sale because neither of the two purchases he identified would have fit into a 2.5 gallon container like the one that was found at the scene. Glenn got around this problem by conveniently claiming that he remembered seeing the individual overfill the can in an effort to round the purchase off to an even number.

Trooper Mason indicates on page 12: 21, of his May 27 report that Glenn brought up the subject of spilled gasoline in his May 18 meeting with Detective Pina while he was being shown the photo array. However, Pina makes no mention of this in his testimony and Glenn specifically stated under cross-examination that he never discussed the subject of spilled gasoline with Detective Pina during their May 18 encounter. (Trial transcript pg. 4-271) Also, when he was asked if he told Detective Pina that the person had short hair, Glenn reiterates that Pina didn't ask him any questions. (Trial transcript pg. 4-276)

Obviously, there in no reason why the allegedly spilled gasoline would have come up in conversation during the May 18 photo identification but there is a very good reason why it would come up during the May 21 cash register tape identification and the fact that Mason would lie about this little detail indicates the likelihood that he had something to hide.

It would be remarkable if Glenn just happened to mention the convenient information to Detective Pina on the 18th as Mason's report suggests but it is far more likely that it was in direct response to the discrepancy on the cash register tape and probably involved some leading on the part of investigators. For example, Mason could have directed Glenn's attention to the 2.68 gallon purchase in favor of the 3 gallon purchase that he first identified while explaining that it was only a 2.5 gallon container that was found and asking if it was possible the individual had ordered 'regular' instead of 'special' and then perhaps spilled some in an effort to round the purchase off to an even number. Glenn, who appeared eager to be involved, would have easily gone along.

While most of their lies went unchallenged, there was one moment during trial where some of Joe Mason's perjurous testimony was impeached when a sibling took the stand to refute his insistence that he never suggested to her that he thought I might be suffering from schizophrenia. (Trial transcript pgs. 4-68 & 6-45) This may be a small detail but it's an important example of his willingness to lie under oath.

There was also a moment during the trial when my attorney raised concerns that some of the samples removed from the scene smelled like gasoline as they were being passed around to the jurors for their personal viewing. (Trial transcript pg. 2-239) It is unclear why the Prosecutor wanted these particular items to be handled by the jurors when other exhibits were simply held up for their viewing but, since they had already tested positive, it would not be surprising for them to have an odor of gasoline. However, it does seem slightly suspicious considering these items were two and a half years old and had been through the state's testing procedure, which theoretically should have removed any trace elements that would produce such odors.

Another example of Trooper Mason's treachery and creative writing practices can be seen in his downplaying and deception regarding interviews with certain witnesses from the Crescent Beach area following the fire. In his 5/27/93 report, Trooper Joe Mason recorded the following:

[23. On May 16, 1993 this officer spoke with Lisa Poule 25 yrs old, 27 Silvershell Ave. Mattapoisett. She stated that from her house

My Story—Jonathan B Taylor

there is a view of the Taylor home. On the morning of the fire she awoke on her own at aprox. 4:50 A.M.. Upon looking out the window, she saw the Taylor house engulfed in flames. She heard screaming which she believes was coming from inside the house. She also observed Mary Mahady standing on the street watching the fire. She then heard approaching sirens and the fire dept. arrived shortly thereafter.

24. On May 16, 1993, this officer spoke with Elizabeth Raposa 34 years old and her housemate Alan Baker 21 yrs old of 4 Silvershell Ave. Both were awake at approx. 4:30 AM on the morning of the fire. Both stated that they heard at approx. 4:30 AM what sounded like screeching tires in the area.]

This is significant because sometime after the trial, two of my sisters met a man at the Warf Tavern in downtown New Bedford who told them that he had been renting a house in the Crescent Beach area of Mattapoisett in May of 1993 and witnessed a black car racing out of that area at a high rate of speed around the time that the fire occurred. He also stated that he reported this information to authorities and never heard from them again. Through recent contact with Elizabeth Raposa, one of my sisters was able to confirm that it was Alan Baker she had spoken to at the Warf Tavern. Ms. Raposa also stated that she heard the vehicle racing by but did not actually see it herself.

My Story—Jonathan B Taylor

Although a car speeding away from an area may not seem very significant under normal circumstances, the timing and location in this particular case are more than a little suspicious. Especially, when you consider the fact that Crescent Beach was a mostly deserted community during that time of year. In fact, we know that the small handful of residents who occupied homes in the area at the time were all interviewed by authorities and none of them reported leaving the area in a black car or having any guests who may have been driving away at that hour. So, this raises the question of what business did this person have in the Crescent Beach area at that time and what was their reason for being there? More importantly, why were they leaving in such a hurry?

This is further evidence of Joe Mason's willingness to manipulate facts in order to make the narrative align with his own devious agenda. Despite the fact that Ms. Raposa heard the vehicle racing by and Alan Baker saw the vehicle driving away, Joe Mason leaves out these important details from his report and says that they merely 'heard what sounded like screeching tires'. He then strategically places this watered down account of their interviews immediately after Lisa Poule's account in, which he writes that 'she heard screaming'. Therefore, anyone who read this report would be left with the false impression that Alan Baker and Elizabeth Raposa weren't really sure what they heard and likely had mistaken the sound of screaming for 'what sounded like screeching tires'.

Unfortunately, the tactic worked and despite being listed as defense witnesses at trial, Elizabeth Raposa and Alan Baker were never called to testify. In fact, they were never even interviewed by my attorney or his investigator for what may have been seen as weak or vague testimony based on Mason's misleading report. The fact that he concealed the true nature of their statements shows that he recognized it as something that could easily be perceived as being connected to the fire.

My Story—Jonathan B Taylor

Author's note:

I would like to take this opportunity to address some of the more troubling revelations made in this text as I turn your attention to the trumpeting elephant that stands menacingly in the room while scratching at the surface and preparing to charge. Of the many disturbing disclosures I've discussed, perhaps none are more unsettling than those surrounding the implication of certain individuals in a string of unsolved serial murders, which may have been orchestrated by a man who the commonwealth has made an entire case against me based on a claim that this person doesn't even exist. To acknowledge his existence now would be to contradict that case against me and expose a legacy of corruption that has metastasized through multiple agencies and administrations over the course of many years. In the alternative, they overlook the obvious and allow a potentially dangerous individual to slip through their fingers and walk free among the masses.

This is not to suggest that authorities ever had a chance of catching the fiendish phantom or linking any of those slippery suspects to an actual crime. In spite of their overtness, the clever culprits will always stay a step ahead of their opponents and remain well beyond the realm of repercussions.

My Story—Jonathan B Taylor

It should also be noted that in spite of the fact that my resurfaced memories may have indicated that certain individuals had prior knowledge of the serial murders years before they occurred, there is no way of knowing who actually committed those horrific crimes. Even though one of those individuals once claimed she would carry out the future killings herself, there is no guarantee that she ever followed through on her pledge aside from the coincidental trail of bodies that turned up just as she had described. Under normal circumstances, a confession is considered to be one of the more compelling forms of evidence but, just because someone claims to have done something doesn't necessarily mean that they did it and whether she would actually take the chance of committing the murders herself and run the risk of being caught in the act or somehow having them traced back to her is an entirely different matter.

I realize that there is no obvious reason for why someone would claim responsibility for a string of serial murders that they didn't commit or how they would have the clairvoyance to know that those crimes would one day occur in the first place but these are exceptional circumstances involving extraordinary individuals who have cleverly concealed themselves in obscurity to avoid detection. I would also point out that, considering the amount of influence that the hypnotist with his master planner persona exhibited over my birth mother, it is just as feasible to suppose that he could have convinced her to commit murder, as to imagine him merely making her admit to it.

Having been a victim of wrongful conviction myself, I would normally never provide circumstantial evidence or suspicious finger pointing at someone who may or may not have committed a crime for fear that it could lead to an innocent person's condemnation. However, the knowledge that these individuals wanted the information to be revealed and the certainty that none of my words could ever be used against them has allowed me to make this unprecedented exception to an otherwise unyielding rule.

As unlikely as it seems, these brazen individuals wanted their roles to be known and what better way to announce their presence and cast a cloud of suspicion upon themselves than through the words of one whose mind has been manipulated by hypnosis. This provides them with a level of protection since the courts have deemed recovered recollections tainted by hypnosis to be unreliable forms of evidence, preventing prosecutors from ever using my resurfaced memories as tools toward their undoing despite the corroborating facts that support some of my assertions.

I know that some may question my motives and wonder why I would reveal such provocative information in a story that is supposed

My Story—Jonathan B Taylor

to be about wrongful conviction and clearing my name. However, this was never about calling out suspects for their alleged crimes or assisting authorities in bringing someone to justice. It was about exposing the truth of what was done to me while simultaneously showing exactly what some of these participants are capable of and just how far they are willing to go.

At one point during the investigation into the Highway Killings, the FBI developed a profile of the killer in the summer of 1989, which described the possible suspect as having 'remarkable appearances'. The Bristol County DA at the time announced, "We have suspects who fit this profile." However, no such suspects were ever named. Several other suspects were publicly identified but none of them appeared to fit the profile. Who were the mysterious suspects who 'fit the profile' and why were their identities kept private while others were so readily revealed?

Over the years, advancements in DNA technology have led to the capture of countless killers in cold cases across the country. By cross-referencing crime scene samples with ancestral DNA sites, authorities have made familial matches that narrowed the scope of their searches and allowed them to zero in on likely suspects. At the very least, it could provide the nationality or ethnicity of a potential suspect. It is unclear if these types of attempts have been made in connection to the

My Story—Jonathan B Taylor

Highway Killings or if investigators are even interested in solving those crimes but it would be curious to see what such results would reveal about the suspect samples that were collected in the infamous string of serial murders. Although, any matches that were made would be called into question by the possibility that those samples were deliberately left behind by the perpetrator as a false lead and the true identity of the Highway Killer may never be known.

If you believe in the phenomena of the light people and the concept that these events are connected to an elaborate test being administered by an unforgiving overlord, then it is easy to imagine those travelers being placed in strategic roles throughout the construct to play predestined parts such as a clueless judge, an unsuspecting juror, a corrupt prosecutor or perhaps even a psychopathic killer.

My Story—Jonathan B Taylor

'A Fight for Freedom'

Have you ever been accused of something you didn't do or suspected someone else of doing something that they didn't do? We've all been in situations where we thought we had it all figured out, only to learn that we had it all wrong when the truth finally came to light.

It is no different for authorities who are forced to make snap assumptions and draw quick conclusions when responding to a call despite being just as much in the dark as the rest of us. Once they arrive on a scene, detectives must first determine if a crime has been committed and then identify a suspect. Placed under enormous public pressure to solve crimes, they often act with haste, which provides the foundation on, which a wrongful conviction may be formed.

Once a suspect has been named, authorities will seldom admit to a mistake even if the evidence begins to suggest otherwise. Whereas most of us can admit we were wrong when we've made a false accusation, authorities can never do this for fear that their entire credibility could then be called into question.

Unfortunately, the way that the justice system works in this country, we are all just a few uncanny coincidences away from a wrongful conviction at any given moment in time. Up against the

My Story—Jonathan B Taylor

unlimited resources of the government, there isn't much that the average person can do in such a situation and sometimes it takes a village to bring the scales of justice back into balance.

*Proceeds from this book will go to my 'fight for freedom' legal defense fund. Thank you for your contribution.

*Full copies of the trial and motions hearings transcripts referenced in this text are public records and may be obtained at any time from the appropriate state agencies.

*If you have questions or comments about the material discussed in this text or have any information related to this case, please contact me at: Jonathan Taylor/ #W-59662/ P O Box 43/ Norfolk, MA 02056 or email me through 'Corrlinks'. (*note: Corrlinks does not forward emails and therefore, requires users to check messages at the site.) Unfortunately, due to the nature of incarceration, all contact information is subject to change. However, any updates or modifications that occur can be obtained through the Massachusetts Department of Corrections website.

*This is an ongoing saga so, please stay tuned...

My Story—Jonathan B Taylor

My Story—Jonathan B Taylor

www.ingramcontent.com/pod-product-compliance
Lightning Source LLC
Chambersburg PA
CBHW052146070526
44585CB00017B/2002